Elite Capture

A WORLD BANK STUDY

Elite Capture

Residential Tariff Subsidies in India

Kristy Mayer, Sudeshna Ghosh Banerjee, and Chris Trimble

WORLD BANK GROUP

Contents

Tables

Foreword

India faces several interlocking challenges as it moves toward achieving electricity access for all of its citizens. At present, power reliability is a major issue. Power infrastructure is underfinanced, and many state-distribution utilities are operating at a loss. In the past decade, substantial efforts have been made to increase affordable access for the poor. Even so, 311 million people, about a quarter of the population, still remain without power. The current national grid program provides capital for new investments, but policy reforms have not kept pace to ensure the poorest households are reached; that households with electricity are provided high-quality, fairly priced service; and that service providers can recover the cost of supply. Addressing these issues requires innovative, mutually reinforcing solutions and policies.

This study focuses on India's residential electricity subsidies, as viewed through a poverty lens. The analysis underscores the country's need to rationalize tariff policies to achieve more equitable subsidy distribution at a far lower cost. Addressing these issues is especially urgent since the residential electricity sector accounts for nearly a quarter of India's total electricity consumption. The results show that most households with electricity receive a net subsidy on their electricity consumption, and subsidies tend to be skewed toward the upper-income groups. Key findings are that 87 percent of subsidy payments are directed to the non-poor instead of households below the poverty line. Regressive tariff policies that result in losses for the utilities are the main reason for this outcome. In 2010, residential subsidies represented 0.4 percent of gross domestic product (GDP), a significant opportunity cost for state governments and their utility companies.

By eliminating subsidy distortions through improved tariff design, along with expanding electricity access to its last-mile customers, India can improve its residential subsidy performance. A greater share of the poorest households stand to benefit from the subsidies, and their cost can remain below current levels. The study highlights sound practices from India's states and model tariff designs that regulators may consider as medium-term policy goals, as well as incremental steps toward reaching them. As the study suggests, however, eliminating subsidies alone will not ensure program success. Other complementary actions are needed. These include promoting more efficient use of electricity and, perhaps more important, building consumer trust by reducing inflated costs and avoidable inefficiencies. With reliable, good-quality electricity, higher consuming households will be willing to accept the tariff increases required to meet the cost of supply.

Jack Stein
Sector Director
South Asia Sustainable Development Department
The World Bank

Elite Capture • http://dx.doi.org/10.1596/978-1-4648-0412-0

Acknowledgments

This study was carried out under the auspices of the India Power Sector Review, led by Sheoli Pargal and Sudeshna Ghosh Banerjee. The core team for this study comprised Kristy Mayer, Sudeshna Ghosh Banerjee, and Chris Trimble.

The authors gratefully acknowledge the advice and suggestions of Technical Advisory Panel members of the India Power Sector Review. They also thank peer reviewers Laurent Durix and Gabriela Inchauste for their valuable suggestions. Also, they extend thanks to Kwawu Gaba, Ashish Khanna, Rohit Mittal, Mohua Mukherjee, and Sheoli Pargal for constructive ideas and discussion at various stages of this work. Norma Adams edited the report.

The authors gratefully acknowledge the financial support provided by the Energy Sector Management Assistance Program, the South Asia Poverty and Social Impact Analysis Trust Fund, and Asia Sustainable and Alternative Energy Program.

Abbreviations

APL	above poverty line
BPL	below poverty line
GDP	gross domestic product
IBT	Increasing Block Tariff
PFC	Power Finance Corporation
RBI	Reserve Bank of India
RGGVY	Rajiv Gandhi Grameen Vidyutikaran Yojana
SERC	State Electricity Regulatory Commission
UID	unique identification
UIDAI	Unique Identification Authority of India
VDT	volume-differentiated tariff

Executive Summary

India—home to one of the world's largest populations without electricity access—has set the ambitious goal of achieving universal electrification by 2017, with a minimum lifeline consumption of 1 kilowatt-hour per household. Like many countries, India subsidizes the electricity tariffs of its low-income households to ensure that utility companies can expand their customer base and that poorer consumers can have ongoing power service. At present, the Government of India extends rural electrification using two instruments: free connections to households below the poverty line (BPL) and consumption subsidies. Under its flagship rural electrification program, Rajiv Gandhi Grameen Vidyutikaran (RGGVY), launched in 2005, BPL households receive free connections, while the consumption of rural, poor, and otherwise low-volume electricity consumers is subsidized in the form of tariffs below cost recovery.

This study analyzes the complex issue of India's residential electricity subsidies, using poverty as a lens to focus on how well subsidies are being targeted to the poor. It centers on subsidies for electricity consumption, examining their size, distribution across household groups, and cost. Primary data for the study is derived mainly from household interviews conducted by the National Sample Survey Organization under the National Sample Survey. The comparison of two survey rounds (2004/05 and 2009/10) was used to assess changes in electricity consumption over time. The study approach analyzed subsidy distribution by both BPL and above poverty line (APL) grouping, as well as income quintile, to allow for the wide variation in poverty rates among states.

The analysis shows that residential tariff structures across India are quite similar. The vast majority of states use an increasing block tariff (IBT) structure, meaning that all households on a given tariff schedule are charged the same low monthly rate for an initial amount of electricity consumption and increasingly higher rates for added consumption blocks. However, states vary widely in how they set tariff levels and treat subsidies. These differences, in turn, complicate the residential subsidy issue, but create opportunities for learning from good practices within India and elsewhere to move toward achieving better subsidy performance.

The research results demonstrate that an overwhelming 87 percent of all residential electricity consumption in India is subsidized, equivalent to more than one-fifth of all electricity consumed in the country in 2010. In addition, residential subsidies are large compared to the cost of electricity and the small cross-subsidy amounts taken from non-subsidized residential consumption. For the 87 percent of subsidized electricity units, the average subsidy is Rs. 1.5 per kilowatt-hour. The average cost of electricity supply is Rs. 3.78 per kilowatt-hour, while the average cross-subsidy is just Rs. 0.62 per kilowatt-hour. Furthermore, the vast majority of households with electricity receive a net subsidy on their electricity consumption.

Key findings are that 87 percent of subsidy payments go to APL households instead of to the poor, and over half of subsidy payments are directed to the richest two-fifths of households. In 2010, the poorest two-fifths of households accounted for just 14 percent and 16 percent, respectively, of subsidy payments. Furthermore, these estimates are conservative because they assume that BPL and APL households are accurately identified. Recent studies show that the misidentification of BPL households has resulted in treating some APL households as BPL households and vice versa. Because APL households tend to consume more electricity, subsides are skewed toward the upper quintiles.

The major driver of these outcomes is tariff design. Few states have highly concessional BPL tariffs. In most, all households are eligible for a subsidy on at least a portion of their monthly electricity consumption. This factor, combined with the fact that the poorest households consume relatively small amounts of electricity, means that wealthier consumers with electricity access are typically eligible for just as much, if not more, subsidy as poorer ones. Because the poorer income quintiles comprise the largest portion of the remaining quarter of India's households without electricity, a relatively larger share of the poor is unable to take advantage of tariff subsidies.

Given that households in India consume nearly one-quarter of the country's electricity, it is not surprising that net residential electricity subsidies—that is, subsidies plus cross-subsidies—represent a significant share of the total subsidy paid by state governments to support the electric utilities. In 2010, residential subsidies totaled Rs. 220,119 million, equal to about or 0.4 percent of gross domestic product (GDP). Even in states where residential electricity subsidies are funded by cross-subsidies from other sectors, such as industry and commerce, residential subsidies still represent a significant opportunity cost for state governments and their utility companies. For comparison purposes, central- and state-level expenditures on health and education in 2012 represented 1 percent and 4 percent of GDP, respectively. Reallocating the 0.4 percent of GDP spent on residential electricity subsidies would significantly increase the budgets of these social programs. Reducing residential subsidies would also increase the financial viability of the distribution utilities.

India's states have a variety of available options for improving their subsidy performance. Certain states model good practices that other states could consider adopting. For example, Punjab, Sikkim, Chattisgarh are among the states that achieve high subsidy targeting and low cost by delivering subsidies largely to

BPL households and counterbalancing the subsidy cost with a small cross-subsidy charged to all APL households.

States may consider four model tariff structures that meet the twin, medium-term policy goals of high subsidy targeting and low cost. These are (i) creating BPL tariff schedules and eliminating subsidies from other schedules, (ii) delivering subsidies through cash transfers instead of tariffs, (iii) creating a volume-differentiated tariff (VDT), and (iv) creating a lifeline tariff and removing subsidies from other tariffs. Deciding on the most effective intervention will depend on the strength of a state's BPL identification and cash-transfer delivery system. For states that can accurately identify BPL households, the best choices are either a subsidized BPL schedule paired with an unsubsidized APL schedule or a cash transfer with completely unsubsidized tariff schedules. Cross-subsidies can also help states to further reduce their subsidy burden.

For most states, full and immediate implementation of these model tariff structures would present a challenge since they would require charging many people that currently benefit from the electricity subsidies cost-recovery or higher prices. Thus, in the near term, states may choose to take incremental steps toward implementing these solutions. Proceeding gradually can help to make subsidy removal feasible. Success also depends on pairing these steps with a strong communications strategy and commitment to consumers that the utilities and state governments are reducing inflated electricity costs, eliminating avoidable inefficiencies, and ultimately improving electricity reliability and quality. Before regulators begin increasing tariffs, the utilities need to develop a roadmap and take steps along the path to improved electricity supply. These actions will increase consumers' willingness to accept the higher tariffs and reduce the costs they must cover.

Elite Capture • http://dx.doi.org/10.1596/978-1-4648-0412-0

CHAPTER 1

Introduction

India—home to the world's largest number of households without electricity—has set the ambitious goal of achieving universal electrification by 2017, envisioning minimum household consumption of 1 kilowatt-hour a day. Today 311 million people in India, including more than half of all households in the poorest income group, live without electricity. India's flagship rural electrification program, Rajiv Gandhi Grameen Vidyutikaran Yojana (RGGVY), launched in 2005, has generally succeeded in expanding electricity adoption. By 2010, the country's electrification rate had reached 74 percent, a 15 percent increase from 2000.

Today the long-term sustainability of the RGGVY program is challenged by the scant revenue being realized from past investments in rural infrastructure. The infrastructure for providing electricity to village lines is underfinanced and unreliable. The utilities' transmission and distribution losses are high, averaging 26 percent (Pargal and Banerjee 2014). Poor power reliability, with daily outages in a range of 2–20 hours, is limiting adoption of electricity in rural areas (Krishnaswamy 2010). In turn, the revenue stream from rural households is insufficient to secure a financially sustainable electricity distribution system.

Setting Residential Tariffs

Like many countries, India subsidizes the electricity tariffs of low-income households to ensure that the utility companies can expand their customer base and that poorer consumers can have ongoing power service. Under the RGGVY program, households below the poverty line (BPL) receive free electricity connections, and the electricity consumption of rural, poor, and otherwise low-volume households is subsidized in the form of tariffs that are below cost recovery. Many countries have long used utility subsidies to promote service affordability among the poor (Komives et al. 2005).

Success in rural electrification not only requires government commitment to reaching low-income customers through well-meaning subsidies. Equally important are implementing and enforcing policies that ensure the long-term financial health of the distribution utilities. These include setting residential consumption tariffs at rational levels that allow the distribution companies to recover their costs and thus have incentive to service rural customers. India's recent policy directives have emphasized the importance of narrowing the large gap between the cost of electricity supply and the revenue being realized. For example, the 2006 National Electricity Tariff Policy calls for the effective and transparent targeting of subsidies. By the end of fiscal year 2010/11, all tariffs—except for those directed at low-consuming households (about 30 kilowatt-hour per month)—were to have been set within 20 percent above or below the average cost of supply. However, subsidy leakages to the non-poor have continued to rise.

Study Goal and Objectives

This study analyzes the complex issue of India's residential electricity subsidies to better understand how to improve subsidy targeting and reduce supplier costs. It uses poverty as a lens through which to examine how residential tariffs are structured by state; the prevalence and magnitude of electricity subsidies; their distribution across households, including the targeting of BPL households; and cost. It also examines best practices from India and elsewhere that state regulators can apply to create a better operating environment for the electric utilities, which in turn, can create better service delivery for consumers. The study also fills a knowledge gap in the literature on residential tariff design in Indian states.[1] Ultimately, the Government of India will decide how subsidies are targeted, and state electricity regulators will set tariffs that reflect that policy. To date, subsidy targeting has focused on BPL households; however, as this study analysis demonstrates, an array of policy choices is possible.

Data Sources

This study relied on several data sources. Primary information on monthly electricity consumption and demographics was extracted from household interviews conducted by the National Sample Survey Organization under the National Sample Survey. In the survey interviews, households reported on the quantity and value of their electricity consumption over the 30 days prior to the survey. Households from across the country were randomly sampled, and two rounds of the survey, 2004/05 and 2009/10, were used in order to assess changes in electricity consumption over time (annex 1A).[2]

Data on the state electricity sectors was provided by the State Electricity Regulatory Commissions (SERCs) and the Power Finance Corporation (PFC). Residential tariff schedules published by the SERCs included such information as per-unit consumption charges, fixed charges, and minimum charges, along with instructions on applying tariffs according to a consumer's consumption level and demographics.[3] The PFC report on the performance of state power utilities provided utility-level data on total expenditure and net input energy for utilities selling directly to consumers (PFC 2011).[4]

Terminology and Key Concepts

Throughout this study, various terms are used to refer to household expenditure and tariff schedules, subsidies, electricity cost, and poverty-related concepts. These terms are defined as follows:

- *Household expenditure.* To calculate total monthly household expenditure, a proxy for monthly income, this analysis takes as given households' reported quantity of monthly electricity consumption in kilowatt-hours (annex 1A). Each household's expenditure is imputed by computing the per-unit charges and adding to that any applicable fixed charges based on the tariff schedule matched to that household. If this amount is less than the applicable minimum charge, the amount necessary to reach the minimum payment is added on to the expenditure calculation and is considered part of the fixed charge for later calculations.

  For example, in Bihar, the expenditure for an urban household above the poverty line (APL) that consumes 101 kilowatt-hour per month would be calculated as follows: $2.15 \times 100 + 2.65 \times 1 + 45 = $ Rs. 262.65 (see tariffs schedules, annex 3A). This amount is above the minimum payment for that schedule (Rs. 52), so Rs. 262.65 would be the household's entire payment.
- *Effective tariff.* This is the variable tariff per unit of consumption, plus any fixed monthly charge or payment needed to reach the minimum bill, averaged over all units of consumption. In the above example, the effective tariff on the first 100 kilowatt-hour of consumption would be $2.15 + (45/101) = $ Rs. 2.6 per kilowatt-hour, and the effective tariff for the 101st kilowatt-hour would be $2.65 + (45/101) = $ Rs. 3.1 per kilowatt-hour.
- *Average effective tariff.* This is a household's total monthly electricity expenditure, divided by its electricity consumption. This is equivalent to taking a consumption-weighted average of the effective tariffs. Continuing with the above example, the average effective tariff for the urban APL household in Bihar would be Rs. $262.65/101 = $ Rs. 2.60.
- *Subsidy and cross-subsidy on electricity units.* This analysis estimates the subsidy or cross-subsidy on an individual unit of electricity by subtracting the effective tariff paid by a household for that unit from the average cost of supply in the household's state. That difference is considered a subsidy if it is positive (that is, if the tariff is less than the cost of supply) and a cross-subsidy if it is negative (that is, if the tariff is greater than the cost of supply). An electricity unit that has a subsidy is considered *subsidized.* An electricity unit that has a cross-subsidy is considered *unsubsidized.*
- *Household subsidy and cross-subsidy.* Household subsidy is estimated by aggregating the subsidy received on subsidized electricity units. A household's total cross-subsidy is computed by aggregating the cross-subsidy paid on unsubsidized units. Using these two figures, households can be divided into four categories: (i) fully subsidized, meaning the household's total cross-subsidy

Elite Capture • http://dx.doi.org/10.1596/978-1-4648-0412-0

is zero; (ii) net subsidized, meaning the amount of subsidy the household receives is greater than the amount of cross-subsidy it pays; (iii) net cross-subsidized, meaning the amount of subsidy the household receives is less than the amount of cross-subsidy it pays; and (iv) not subsidized, meaning the household's total subsidy is zero.

- *Subsidy incidence with and without accounting for cross-*subsidies. To examine the benefits incidence of subsidies, the study considers how total subsidy payments are distributed across income quintiles, whereby households are evenly divided into five groups according to total monthly consumption, with the poorest 20 percent falling into the first quintile and the richest 20 percent into the fifth quintile. Subsidy incidence across income quintiles is estimated by summing the total subsidy received by each household in a given quintile and dividing that amount by the total subsidy received by all households. Thus, subsidy incidence describes the percent of all subsidy payments received by all households in a particular quintile.

  To account for cross-subsidies in the subsidy incidence, each household's net subsidy is computed by subtracting its total cross-subsidy from its total subsidy. These net subsidies are then summed across all households in a given quintile, and that sum is divided by the sum of the positive subsidies received by all households across all quintiles. Quintiles in which, in aggregate, households paid more in cross-subsidies than they received in subsidies would have a negative incidence, which represents the percent of the total positive subsidies that quintile funded.

- *Subsidy targeting.* This analysis divides households into below poverty line (BPL) and above poverty line (APL), defined according to their total household monthly expenditure and official poverty thresholds for rural and urban consumption (Planning Commission 2012). Subsidy targeting is defined as the percent of total subsidy payments going to households living below the poverty line. This is computed by summing the subsidy received by households defined as BPL in each state and dividing it by the summation of subsidies received by all households.

- *Cost.* This is the total cost faced by a state's utilities, divided by the amount of energy they purchase. The cost of supplying different households at different times may vary (for example, rural supply is costlier than urban supply, and peak-time consumption is more expensive than at other times). Thus, regulators should consider more specific costs, discovered through a detailed cost-of-supply study, when setting tariffs.

- *Gross cost of the average subsidy.* This figure is computed by first calculating the average subsidy received by all households with electricity access (including households that have access but receive zero subsidies) in each quintile and each state. That average is multiplied by the number of households with electricity access in 2010 in each quintile of each state. The number of households with electricity access is computed by applying the electricity access rates computed in this study to the state's 2010 population.

- *Net cost of the average subsidy*. This figure is computed by calculating the average cross-subsidy paid by all households with electricity access (including households that have access but pay zero cross-subsidies) in each quintile of each state. This state-wise average is multiplied by the number of households with electricity access in 2010 in each quintile of each state. This figure is considered the *revenue from cross-subsidies*. That figure is then subtracted from the gross cost to arrive at the net cost.

Targeting the Poor

In 2010, the poverty rate across India—that is, the share of the country's BPL population—was 29.8 percent. Figure 1.1 shows that BPL households comprised the poorest income quintile and about half of the second income quintile.

This study analyzes subsidy delivery by BPL/APL grouping, as well as by income quintile distribution. This nuanced approach allows for the wide variation in poverty rates among states. For example, in Goa, the poverty rate is only 8.7 percent, compared to 53.5 percent in Bihar.[5]

Structure of This Report

This report has seven chapters. Chapter 2 profiles India's electricity consumption and recent subsidy and cost trends. Chapter 3 describes the tariff structures and schedules used across states. Chapter 4 covers the size and distribution of subsidies across household groups, while chapter 5 focuses on the issue of subsidy targeting. Chapter 6 considers the estimated cost of residential subsidies in the context of electricity-sector and state expenditures. Finally, chapter 7 presents good practices from India, model tariff designs to consider in the medium term, and incremental steps that states can take now toward achieving well-targeted, low-cost subsidies.

Figure 1.1 BPL and APL Households across India, by Income Quintile, 2010

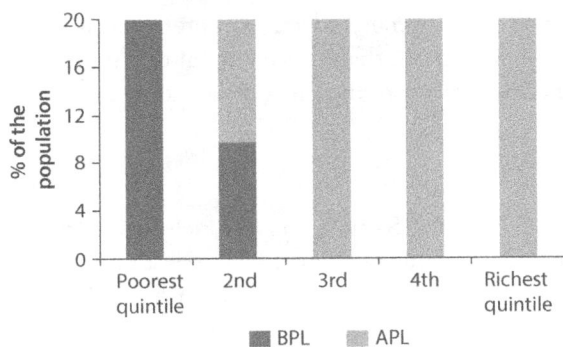

Sources: National Sample Survey 2010; Planning Commission 2012.
Note: APL = above poverty line; BPL = below poverty line.

Annex 1A: National Sample Survey Description

The household-level data used in this study is based on interviews conducted under two rounds of the National Sample Survey (2004/05 [round 60] and 2009/10 [round 66]). Each year, the National Sample Survey Organization conducts consumer expenditure surveys. Household from across India are randomly sampled for interviewing. In the surveys, households report on the quantity and value of their consumption over the "last 30 days" prior to the surveys. The electricity expenditure information and all other data used in this analysis are found in the survey's household consumer expenditure schedule (Schedule 1.0).

Survey Sample
The 2009/10 survey round covered 98,908 households living in Delhi or the 28 states (other union territories were excluded from the analysis). Of this number, 1,991 households or 2 percent of the sample were dropped for reporting errors. (These households reported consuming exactly 1 kilowatt-hour of electricity in the prior month, which is a somewhat implausible value.) The 2004/05 survey round covered 25,253 households living in 20 states (including Delhi). The 2009/10 round included 81,999 households living in the same 20 states; of those, 7 (0.02 percent) were dropped for having reported implausible amounts of electricity consumption.

Calculation Methods
For the remaining households—96,917 in the 2009/10 survey round and 25,246 in the 2004/05 round—this analysis combined the quantity of reported monthly electricity consumption (in kilowatt-hours) with tariff data to impute electricity expenditures (both per kilowatt-hour and in total) (annex 1B).

   An alternate method would have been to combine the reported monthly electricity expenditure (in rupees) with tariff data to impute consumption quantity, and use that figure to impute per-unit expenditures. Although reported expenditures are often more accurate than reported consumption, the latter is preferable for this analysis because it allows for a more accurate application of tariffs to households since tariffs vary with consumption in a variety of ways. It permits the application of a consistent method for both metered and unmetered households;[6] and reported expenditures can include more than just payment due for electricity consumption in a given month (for example, missed payments from other months or meter rent).

Additional Survey Variables
Other variables drawn from the National Sample Survey included state, geographic location (urban or rural), total monthly per-capita expenditure, and survey weights. The monthly per-capita expenditure was used to determine each household's poverty status, using the 2004/05 and 2009/10 poverty lines from the Planning Commission's poverty estimates (Planning Commission 2007, 2012), and to divide households into income quintiles.

Elite Capture • http://dx.doi.org/10.1596/978-1-4648-0412-0

The analysis also used the National Sample Survey to impute household metering status and connected electricity load, neither of which the survey directly reported. Households that in 2005 were located in districts with access rates below 60 percent were assumed to be unmetered since it is likely those districts were unmetered in 2005 and have remained so. Connected load was imputed by dividing monthly electricity consumption by an estimated number of hours of effective consumption per month (representing how often households tend to use their connection in a day). The monthly estimates used for rural and urban households were 120 hours and 300 hours, respectively, taking into account the often limited supply of electricity in rural areas.

Annex 1B: Technical Note on Matching Households and Tariff Schedules

Underlying all of the calculations in this study is the key step of matching households with appropriate tariff rates. This annex describes the assumptions made in the matching process and their limitations.

Key Assumptions

The analysis uses households' reported quantity of monthly electricity consumption (in kilowatt-hours), their location (state and whether urban or rural), poverty status, imputed metering status, and imputed connected load to determine which tariffs apply to them, based on instructions in the states' tariff schedules. To do this, a crucial assumption was made that all electricity consumption is billed exactly as indicated in the tariff schedule.

It is important to note that this means assuming that all households the study has categorized as BPL and that meet the other criteria in the tariff schedule (for example, limit on total electricity consumption) receive the BPL or Kutir Jyoti tariff, if one is specified. It also means that no APL households receive this tariff. Since BPL tariffs are always lower than the corresponding APL tariffs (table 3.3), that assumption potentially leads to overestimating the subsidies going to BPL consumers and underestimating those going to APL consumers. Box 5.1 explains why this assumption may not hold true and recalculates the study's key findings under an alternate assumption.

Another implication of the broad assumption that all electricity consumption is billed exactly as indicated in the tariff schedule is assuming that all electricity consumption is paid for. In reality, the utilities often do not collect all of their bills. For example, collection rates in 2010 ranged from 61 percent to over 100 percent (in cases where the utilities collected on unpaid bills from the previous year) (PFC 2011). If bills were systematically undercollected from certain types of households, this would have led to underestimating the subsidy those households received; however, there is no evidence whether or to what extent this might have occurred.

Notes

1. Similar studies on electricity tariffs and subsidies have been conducted in such countries as Pakistan (Trimble, Yoshida, and Saqib 2011), Bangladesh (Ahmed, Trimble, and Yoshida 2012), and the Maldives (Trimble and Redaelli 2012). Other relevant subsidy studies in South Asia include Rao (2012), which examined kerosene subsidies in India; Fukumi (2012), which analyzed agricultural subsidies in India; and Foster, Pattanayak, and Prokopy (2003), which focused on water subsidies in South Asia.

2. All of the National Sample Survey data used in this analysis are located in the survey's household consumer expenditure schedule (Schedule 1.0).

3. States used 2010 tariff schedules where available, and 2011 schedules otherwise (for example, Goa, Manipur, and Mizoram).

4. The average cost of electricity supply by state was computed by aggregating the expenditure and energy variables by state, and then dividing total expenditures by net input energy.

5. Given the few observations in the samples of some smaller states, this study did not consider divisions at the decile level, which would have made calculations at that level potentially unreliable.

6. Since unmetered households pay only fixed charges, there is no way to impute quantity or per-unit expenditures from the expenditures they report; thus, reported consumption must be used for such households.

CHAPTER 2

Patterns of Residential Consumption and Subsidy and Cost Trends

Given the critical importance of rational tariff policies to achieving a sustainable electrification program, this chapter begins by profiling the electricity consumption patterns of India's residential sector. It then reviews recent trends in subsidy incidence and cost since the Rajiv Gandhi Grameen Vidyutikaran Yojana (RGGVY) program was launched in 2005 to better grasp how well subsidies are being targeted since key policy milestones and funding mandates were instituted.

Residential Sector Profile

India's residential sector accounts for nearly a quarter of the country's total electricity consumption (figure 2.1a). This figure represents one-fifth of the distribution utilities' total revenue (figure 2.1b).

India's large consumer group for residential electricity has ample room for further expansion, which would substantially increase the utilities' customer base. Some 311 million people—about a quarter of the population—still lack access to electricity.[1] About 93 percent of these people live in rural areas, and more than two-thirds are in the lowest 40 percent of the income distribution. About 83 percent reside in five states: Uttar Pradesh, Bihar, West Bengal, Rajasthan, and Orissa. Figure 2.2 shows that Bihar and Uttar Pradesh have the lowest access rates, at just 25 percent and 47 percent, respectively.

Patterns in household electricity consumption vary substantially by income quintile. In 2010, the average household consumed 76 kilowatt-hour a month. Those in the richest income group consumed 2.5 times more electricity than the poorest consumers (121 kilowatt-hour and 45 kilowatt-hour, respectively). The richest 20 percent of households accounted for 38 percent of residential electricity consumption, 15 percent higher than the combined consumption of the poorest 40 percent of households. Average monthly electricity consumption

Figure 2.1 Electricity Consumption and Revenue to Utilities, by Sector, 2010

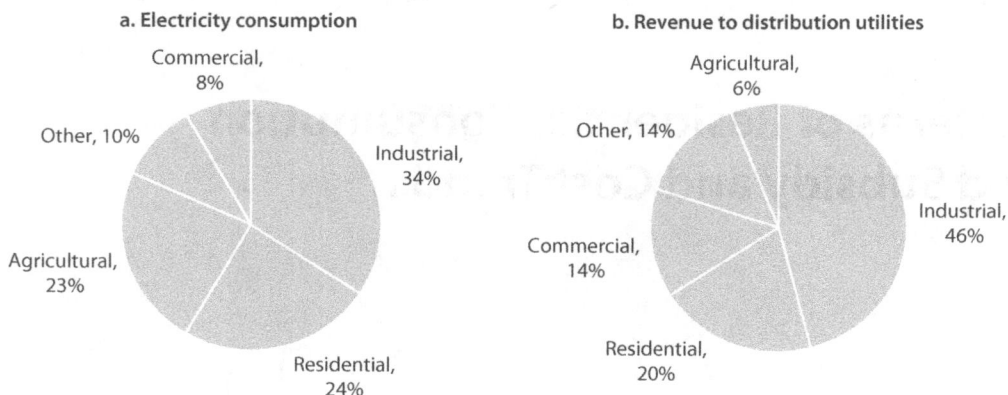

a. Electricity consumption

Commercial, 8%
Other, 10%
Industrial, 34%
Agricultural, 23%
Residential, 24%

b. Revenue to distribution utilities

Agricultural, 6%
Other, 14%
Commercial, 14%
Industrial, 46%
Residential, 20%

Source: PFC 2011.

Figure 2.2 Electricity Access Rates for Selected States, 2010

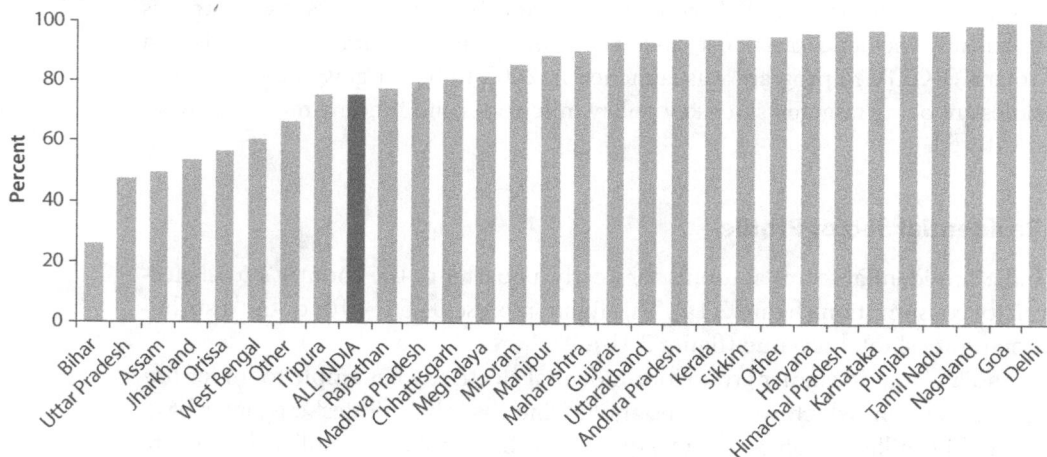

Source: National Sample Survey 2010.

varied significantly between rural and urban areas, as well as between states (appendix A).

More than half of households consume 30–100 kilowatt-hour per month, representing 45 percent of total residential electricity consumption. One-quarter of households consume just 30 kilowatt-hour or less each month, accounting for 7 percent of consumption. Another 17 percent of households consume 100–300 kilowatt-hour per month, representing 36 percent of consumption. Finally, 12 percent of residential consumption is represented by 1 percent of households, who consume more than 300 kilowatt-hour a month.

Subsidy and Cost Trends

Since setting universal electricity access as a national priority, including the targeting of below poverty line (BPL) households, subsidy incidence has improved slightly, as access rates have increased. Among the 20 states analyzed, subsidy leakage to the highest income quintile fell by 6 percent (from 37 percent to 31 percent) between 2005 and 2010. Over that same period, the total subsidy payments received by the poorest income quintile grew by 4 percent (from 10 percent to 14 percent) (figure 2.3). Appendix B shows how the figures varied by state in 2005.

The improvement in subsidy incidence between the survey years was negated by an alarming rise in the average subsidy cost. In real terms, the net cost of the average household subsidy in 2010 was more than 70 times larger than in 2005 (figure 2.4). For the 20 states covered in the analysis, the net cost in 2005 was Rs. 1,847 million. By 2010, it had climbed to Rs. 131,569 million (in 2005 rupees) (appendix B).[2]

The combined impact of the slight improvement in subsidy incidence and significant cost increase is reflected in the change in size and share of costs attributable to BPL and APL consumers over the five-year period. In 2005, subsidies

Figure 2.3 Recent Trend in Subsidy Incidence, by Income Quintile

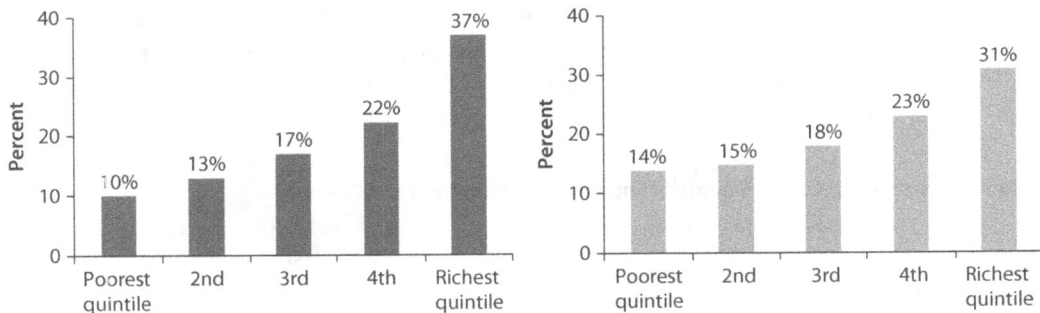

Sources: National Sample Survey 2005, 2010; PFC 2005, 2010; SERCs 2005, 2010.

Figure 2.4 Rapid Rise in Average Subsidy Cost

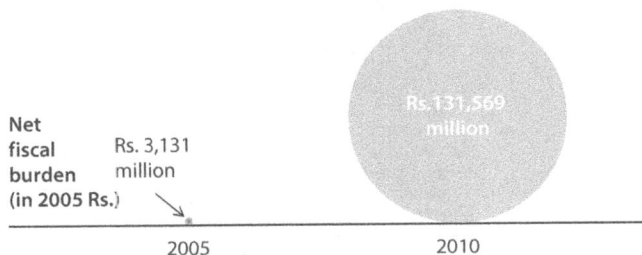

Sources: National Sample Survey 2005, 2010; PFC 2005, 2010; SERCs 2005, 2010; Planning Commission.
Note: 2010 value is limited to the 20 states for which 2005 data were available.

Elite Capture • http://dx.doi.org/10.1596/978-1-4648-0412-0

for BPL households totaled Rs. 178 million, while subsidies for APL households totaled Rs. 1,669 million or about 90 percent of the total cost. More than two-fifths of the APL subsidies (Rs. 683 million) went to the richest 20 percent of households. In 2010, BPL households received Rs. 17,790 million (in 2005 rupees), a 100-fold increase over 2005 receipts, while APL households received Rs. 113,779 million, a 68-fold increase over 2005. Thus, even though the subsidy receipts of BPL households climbed notably more than those of APL households, the latter group accounted for the bulk of the residential subsidy cost.

The significant expansion in residential subsidies in 2005–10 was offset only somewhat by cross-subsidies from other electricity sectors (for example, industrial or commercial consumers). For the 20 states analyzed, the total net subsidies requested by the distribution companies from the state governments more than doubled over the five-year period (from Rs. 114,389 million to Rs. 241,661 million).

The changes in subsidy targeting and cost in 2005–10 were driven by an increase in the real cost of electricity supply, coupled with a decrease in the real value of tariffs, as well as increased electricity access rates and higher electricity consumption. A real increase in the average cost of electricity supply increased the average subsidy cost, although it reduced subsidy leakage by raising the cost of supply above the effective tariffs for some poor consumers that paid a high fixed cost. For India overall, the average cost of supply rose by 59 percent in nominal terms, but just 13 percent in real terms (figure 2.5a). At the state level, changes in the real cost of supply varied significantly. Twelve states experienced increases ranging from 3 percent (Gujarat) to 78 percent (Maharashtra), while the other eight saw decreases ranging from 4 percent (Karnataka) to 57 percent (Assam).

Figure 2.5 Increasing Cost of Electricity Supply and Falling Tariffs, 2005–10

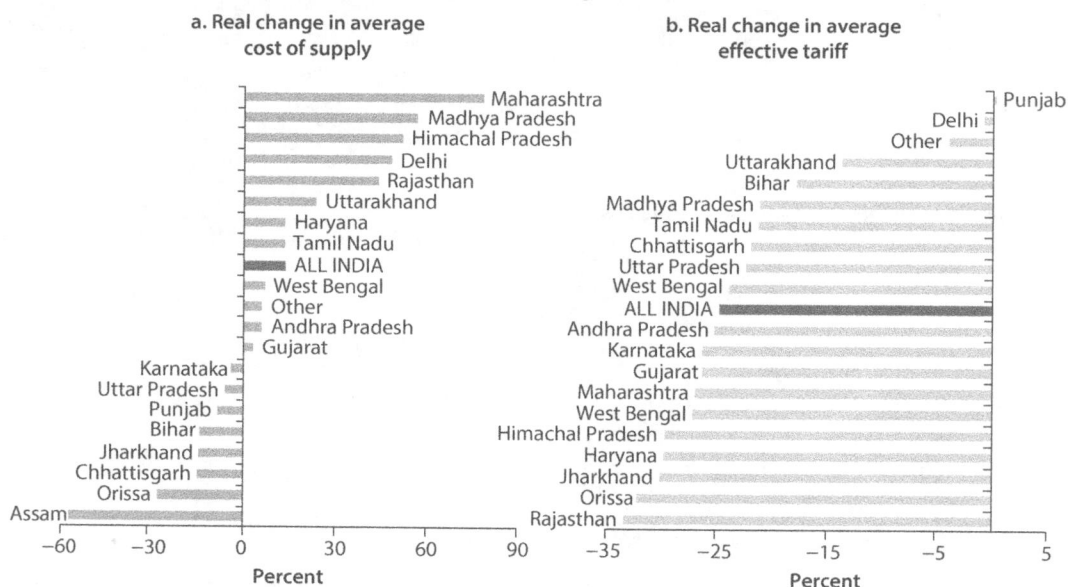

Sources: National Sample Survey 2005, 2010; PFC 2005, 2010; SERCs 2005, 2010.

By allowing tariffs to fall relative to inflation, states drastically increased the cost of subsidies. This decision, which increased the amount of subsidy leakage to the non-poor, proved quite costly. Over the period, the average effective tariff rose by 6 percent in nominal terms; however, in real terms, it fell by 25 percent. In 17 of the 20 states analyzed, the average effective tariff fell by more than 10 percent in real terms (figure 2.5b).

The expansion in electricity access was concentrated in the poorest quintiles, which decreased subsidy leakage to the non-poor and minimally increased the cost of supply. Access rates increased by 12 percentage points in the poorest quintile, compared to 6 percentage points in the richest quintile. The number of poor households receiving subsidies increased substantially, while richer households saw a slight increase (figure 2.6). Expanding access to more households had the dual effect of increasing subsidy payments to the poor and reducing subsidy leakage to the non-poor. It also increased the cost, but the impact was minimal since most access gains were among low-consuming households that received relatively small subsidies.

Higher consumption in each quintile resulted in an improved cost of supply (holding constant 2005 values for tariffs, costs, and access) and a slight reduction in subsidy leakage to the non-poor. Consumption by quintile figures prominently in subsidy incidence and cost. In the lower quintiles, it determines how much of the available subsidies the poorest households can take advantage of, while in the upper quintiles, it determines how much of the cross-subsidies the richest households can accrue. In 2005–10, the average electricity consumption among connected households in the poorest quintile grew from 41 kilowatt-hour to 45 kilowatt-hour per month. Among the richest households, it increased from 102 kilowatt-hour to 121 kilowatt-hour a month (figure 2.7). These changes in consumption patterns increased the amount of subsidized electricity that the poorest households consumed and added to the states' cross-subsidy revenues from the richest households.

Figure 2.6 Change in Electricity Access Rates, by Income Quintile, 2005 and 2010

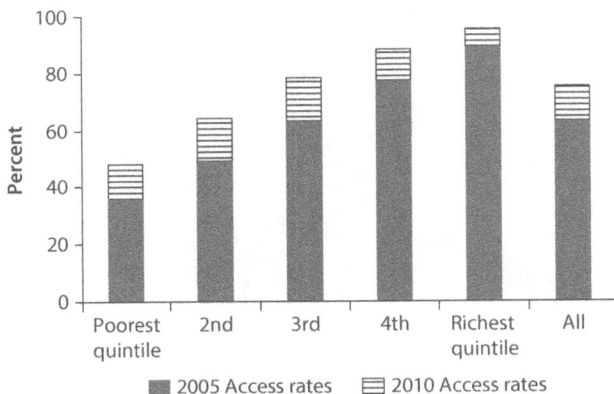

Source: National Sample Survey 2005, 2010.

Elite Capture • http://dx.doi.org/10.1596/978-1-4648-0412-0

Figure 2.7 Change in Average Electricity Consumption, by Income Quintile, 2005 and 2010

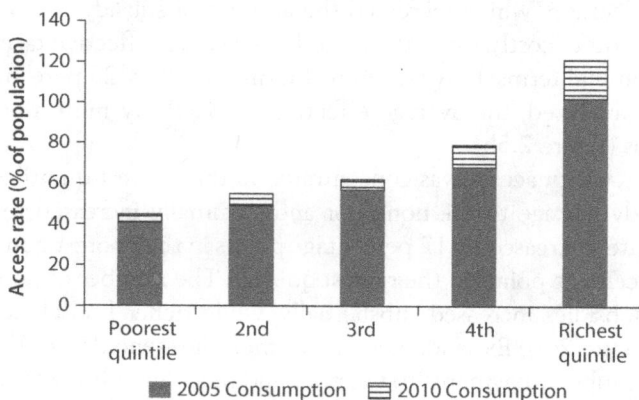

Source: National Sample Survey 2005, 2010.

Notes

1. In this study, a household is assumed to have electricity access if it reported positive, nonzero electricity consumption in the month of the National Sample Survey (the most relevant measure for calculating electricity subsidies). In the 2009/10 survey round, 18 percent of the sample (17,401 households) reported no electricity consumption, compared to 32 percent (8,062 households) in the 2004/05 round.

2. The analysis of changes that occurred between survey years was limited to 20 states; nine states for which 2005 tariff schedules were available were not included (including Goa, Kerala, Manipur, Meghalaya, Mizoram, Nagaland, Sikkim, and Tripura).

CHAPTER 3

Residential Tariffs Overview

Residential tariff structures across India are similar, but states differ widely in the ways they set tariff levels and treat subsidies. This chapter begins by describing the prevalent residential tariff structures used in India. It then turns to key features of tariff schedules, the array of state-level variations, and finally the effects of certain features on poor electricity consumers.

Tariff Structures

The vast majority of states in India use an increasing block tariff (IBT) structure—the world's most widely used form of consumption subsidy (Komives et al. 2005). Under the IBT structure, all households on a given tariff schedule are charged the same low monthly rate for initial electricity consumption and increasingly higher rates for added consumption blocks. In Bihar, for example, all above poverty line (APL) households living in urban areas are charged Rs. 2.15 per kilowatt-hour for the first 100 kilowatt-hour of electricity consumed; households consuming above that amount are charged the same low rate for the first 100 kilowatt-hour, plus Rs. 2.65 per kilowatt-hour for the amount consumed in the next block (100–200 kilowatt-hour). State variations in the number of consumption blocks are in a one–eight range, averaging about three (figure 3.1a). For states with only one block, consumption begins at 25 kilowatt-hour, and there is no upper limit. For most states, the cutoff for the initial consumption block falls between about 30 kilowatt-hour and 100 kilowatt-hour. For the last consumption block, the cut-off range is 200–400 kilowatt-hour (figure 3.1b).

A less commonly used tariff structure in India is the volume-differentiated tariff (VDT). Under the VDT structure, households pay the same rate for all kilowatt-hours of consumption; that is, the rate depends on total consumption. For example, in Chhattisgarh, which uses the VDT, any household consuming up to 200 kilowatt-hour a month would pay Rs. 1.6 per kilowatt-hour, while a household consuming 200–500 kilowatt-hour a month would pay Rs. 1.9 per kilowatt-hour (including the initial 200 kilowatt-hour of consumption).

Figure 3.1 Features of Increasing Block Tariff, 2010

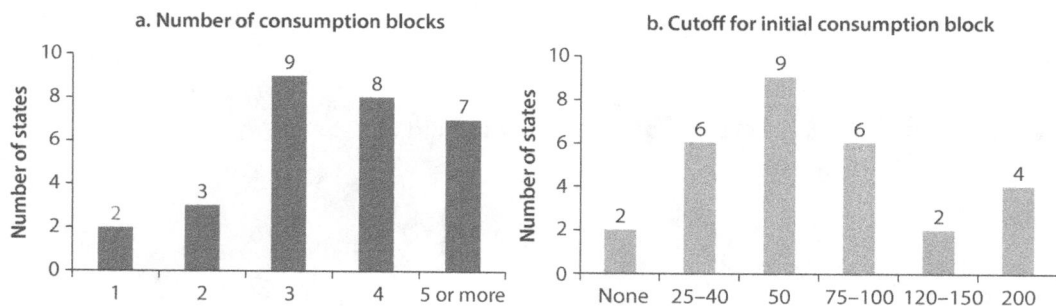

Source: SERCs 2010.

Tariff Schedule Characteristics

Most states in India set their own tariff schedules, which vary substantially (annex 3A).[1] In addition to charging for the kilowatt-hours consumed,[2] tariff schedules often include lump-sum payments in the form of fixed charges that all households pay and/or minimum payments that all customers must meet, either by accruing enough consumption charges or making lump-sum payments on top of consumption charges. Figure 3.2 shows the share of states that implement each of these variations under the IBT structure. Fixed and minimum charges may vary by connection type (for example, size of connected load or single- versus three-phase load); more often, households on a given schedule are charged the same.

Lump-sum payments are levied because marginal cost pricing is insufficient to meet the full cost of production. These costs generally originate from (i) the high share of fixed cost in the total cost, (ii) the high share of non-attributable or common costs in the total cost, and/or (iii) the high capital intensity of creating electricity-sector assets that require lump-sum capital investments and long gestation periods (Komives et al. 2005). In such situations, lump-sum payments are used to capture the fixed cost of supply and achieve full-cost recovery.

To better align residential electricity tariffs with the needs of a growing consumer base and promote affordability among the poorest households, most states segment their schedules by consumers' poverty status and geographic location. These two categories reflect the respective capacities of below the poverty line (BPL) and APL households to pay for electricity and urban/rural differences in supply quality and availability. Some states create tariff schedules based on metering, connected load (that is, kilowatt size or single- versus three-phase), or total electricity consumption. Table 3.1 suggests the potential range of variations among state schedules, using Andhra Pradesh and Bihar as examples. Andhra Pradesh has a single schedule for all households with a tariff and minimum payment but no fixed charge. By contrast, Bihar has six schedules that account for rural/urban, APL/BPL, load size, and metering differences.

Elite Capture • http://dx.doi.org/10.1596/978-1-4648-0412-0

Figure 3.2 Types of IBT Schedules Implemented by States, 2010

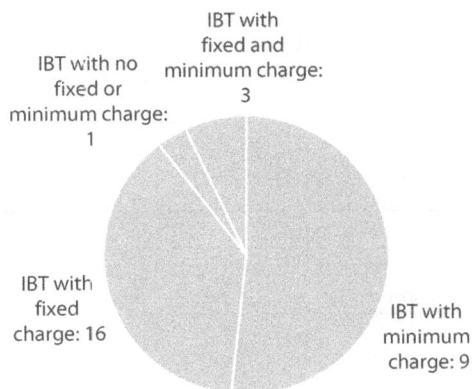

IBT with no fixed or minimum charge: 1

IBT with fixed and minimum charge: 3

IBT with fixed charge: 16

IBT with minimum charge: 9

Source: World Bank.
Note: IBT = increasing block tariff.

Table 3.1 Examples of State Tariff Schedules Used in This Analysis

State	Consumer group	Minimum payment	Fixed charge	Tariff per kWh of consumption (Rs.) (kWh range to which tariff applies)				
Andhra Pradesh	All	25	0	1.45	2.8	3.05	4.75	5.5
				(0–50)	(51–100)	(101–200)	(201–300)	(301+)
Bihar	urban; Rural > 2 kW	40 for 1 kW; 20/kW added	45 for <= 3 kW	2.15	2.65	3.2	4	
				(0–100)	(101–200)	(201–300)	(301+)	
	Rural < 2 kW	52 for 1 kW; 81 for 2 kW	0	1.3	1.55	1.75		
				(0–50)	(51–100)	(101+)		
	Rural, unmetered	0	80 for 1 kW of connected load; 120 for > 1 kW of connected load; no variable rate					
	Urban BPL[a]	35	0	1.5				
				(0–30)				
	Rural BPL, metered[a]	25	0	1.2				
				(0–30)				
	Rural BPL, unmetered	0	35	no variable rate				

Source: SERCs 2010.
Note: Excerpted from annex 3A. BPL = below the poverty line; kW = kilowatt; kWh = kilowatt-hour.
a. BPL consumers are eligible for this schedule only if their total consumption in a given month is less than 30 kilowatt-hour.

The types and number of residential tariff schedules used by states vary wide-ly (table 3.2). In 19 states, tariffs are set lower for BPL or Kutir Jyoti consum-ers, although eligibility for the lower rates often depends on keeping monthly electricity consumption below a certain threshold (usually 30 kilowatt-hour) (box 3.1). Four states use lifeline rates for BPL and APL households. Nine states distinguish between urban and rural areas. Another 22 states differentiate between connection type, charging a higher fixed or minimum rate or higher consumption charge for larger connected loads or three-phase connections. In two states (Andhra Pradesh and Haryana), households are charged according the same tariff schedule. Finally, nine states use fixed-charge-only tariffs for unmetered households.

Table 3.2 Residential Tariff Schedule Types, 2010

State	Differentiating factors for tariff schedules				Number of tariff schedules
	Urban/rural	BPL/APL	Total electricity consumption	Connection type	
Andhra Pradesh					1
Haryana					1
Delhi				•	2
Nagaland				•	2
Sikkim				•	2
Rajasthan	•				2
Himachal Pradesh		•			2
Meghalaya		•			2
Goa		•			2
Other				•	2
Tamil Nadu		•	•		3
Kerala		•		•	3
Maharashtra		•		•	3
Orissa		•		•	3
Punjab		•		•	3
Assam		•		•	3
Chhattisgarh		•		•	3
Manipur		•		•	3
Mizoram		•		•	3
Uttarakhand		•		•	3
Other		•		•	3
Madhya Pradesh	•		•	•	4
Uttar Pradesh	•		•	•	4
Gujarat	•	•		•	4
Tripura	•	•		•	4
Bihar	•	•		•	4
Jharkhand	•	•		•	4
Karnataka	•	•		•	4
West Bengal	•	•	•	•	4

Source: SERCs 2010.
Note: • indicates factor is used to distinguish between tariff schedules. APL = above poverty line; BPL = below poverty line.

How Fixed Charges Impact the Poor

Because of the array of influencing factors (for example, poverty, demographics, consumption, and metering), the prices residential consumers pay per unit of electricity vary widely by state. Thus, this analysis computes the average effective tariff (that is, the weighted average of consumption charges and fixed or minimum charges over a household's total consumption units). The results show that the average tariffs paid by APL consumers range from less than Rs. 1 per kilowatt-hour (in Jharkhand) to more than Rs. 4 per kilowatt-hour (in Uttar Pradesh). In several states (Punjab, Meghalaya, and Kerala), some BPL consumers receive free electricity; while in Rajasthan, some BPL consumers pay as much as Rs. 4.6 per kilowatt-hour. It appears that fixed charges have a dramatic effect on low-volume consumers. Indeed, in many states, low-consuming APL households—and, in some states, BPL households—pay a higher tariff per unit of electricity than do high-consuming APL households.

Box 3.1 Snapshot of BPL Tariff Programs

India's 2005 National Electricity Policy suggests that residential subsidies should be directed to households that consume small amounts of electricity (for example, up to 30 kilowatt-hour a month) and limited to half the cost of supply. As early as 1979, Karnataka and many other states offered BPL consumers lower tariffs. In the late 1980s, the Kutir Jyoti program provided all BPL consumers single-point light connections, using a 100-percent grant for connection charges, although the program had no official stance on BPL tariffs. Today, BPL tariff programs vary widely across states. As of 2010, 19 states—68 percent of all states—charged BPL households lower tariffs. Six states limited BPL tariffs to households with a maximum consumption of 30 kilowatt-hour a month. In another seven states, the BPL tariff range was 15–200 kilowatt-hour of monthly consumption. Effective subsidy rates also vary substantially. Most states do not comply with the 2005 subsidy policy directive. Out of the 19 state tariff programs that charge BPL consumers lower rates, 14 are 51–100 below cost recovery. Tariff schedules in some states assume that eligible BPL households are identified through holding BPL cards, but recent studies show that the misallocation of BPL cards is resulting in subsidy leakage (box 5.1).

Source: World Bank.

Figure 3.3 provides an example of how a tariff schedule with an IBT structure and a fixed charge translates into average effective tariffs that vary based on total monthly consumption. An IBT-structured tariff schedule with a minimum charge would generate a similar consumption curve.

Table 3.3 compares the average effective tariff for two representative consumption levels (30 kilowatt-hour[3] and 75 kilowatt-hour[4]) for urban, rural, and rural unmetered BPL (30 kilowatt-hour only) and APL consumers. Thirteen states have various types of APL consumers who pay different average prices to

Figure 3.3 Example of Average Effective Tariffs, 2010

a. Tariff per consumption unit

b. Overall average tariff for household with given monthly consumption

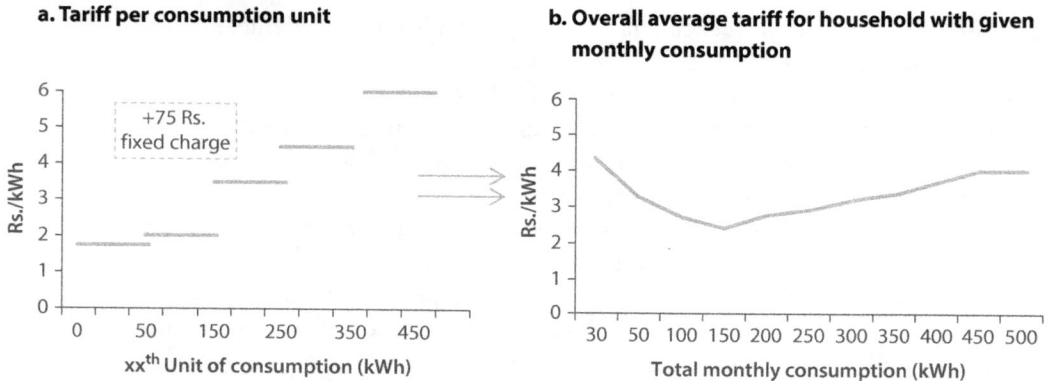

Source: World Bank.

consume 75 kilowatt-hour. Such price differentiation is less common for BPL consumers; in only 10 states do different BPL consumers pay different prices to consume 30 kilowatt-hour, and often that difference is driven by metering status. BPL consumers pay average tariffs ranging from Rs. 0 in Punjab and Meghalaya (this permits free consumption for BPL households that consume less than 200 kilowatt-hour and 30 kilowatt-hour, respectively) to Rs. 4.62 in Rajasthan. The difference between APL and BPL tariffs is the highest in Maharashtra, Meghalaya, and Punjab, where APL consumers may pay more than Rs. 2 per kilowatt-hour more than do BPL customers. Consumers that are unmetered often pay more (including in Mizoram, Uttar Pradesh, and Uttarakhand) since utilities charge them the same fixed cost regardless of the amount consumed.

Notably, in some states, BPL and APL households that consume only 30 kilowatt-hour per month—four states for BPL and 14 for APL consumers—pay more per kilowatt-hour than do similar APL households in the same geographic area that consume 75 kilowatt-hour a month. The fixed and/or minimum charges in most states' tariff schedules account for this anomaly. Households must pay the fixed charge regardless of the amount of electricity they consume. Thus, by design, the average effective tariff is raised more on low-consuming households than on high-consuming ones. Similarly, all households must pay a minimum charge, either by accruing enough per-unit charges or making a lump-sum payment on top of their per-unit charges. This means only relatively low-consuming households must make lump-sum payments.

Fixed and minimum charges have a stark impact on low-consuming households (that is, those who consume less than 30 kilowatt-hour per month) or 29 percent of all BPL households. In 21 states, the average low-consuming household pays more per kilowatt-hour of electricity than does the average household that consumes 30–100 kilowatt-hour per month. In 10 of those states (Bihar, Delhi, Haryana, Himachal Pradesh, Jharkhand, Manipur, Orissa, Rajasthan,

Table 3.3 Average Effective Tariff for Representative Monthly Consumption Levels, 2010

State	BPL, 30 kWh			APL, 30 kWh			APL, 75 kWh		
	Urban	Rural	Unmetered	Urban	Rural	Unmetered	Urban	Rural	Unmetered
Andhra Pradesh		1.45			1.45			1.90	
Assam		2.85			4.00			3.40	
Bihar	1.50	1.20	1.17	3.65	1.73	2.67	2.75	1.38	1.07
Chhattisgarh	1.50		1.67		1.60			1.60	
Delhi		3.25			3.25			2.77	
Goa		0.80			1.60			1.82	
Gujarat		1.67		2.87		2.37	2.87		2.37
Haryana		2.67			2.67			3.10	
Himachal Pradesh		0.70			1.53			1.03	
Jharkhand	1.00		0.90	2.02	1.00	2.17	1.62	1.00	0.87
Karnataka		0.74		2.52	2.18		2.75		2.61
Kerala		1.15[a]			1.15			1.50	
Madhya Pradesh	2.65		2.82	2.62		2.82	3.17	3.10	1.13
Maharashtra		0.76			3.35			2.75	
Manipur	1.92		1.17	4.20		9.33	3.00		3.73
Meghalaya		0.00			3.08			2.58	
Mizoram	1.31		0.78	2.33		3.33	1.95		1.33
Nagaland		2.33			2.33			2.66	
Orissa		1.00			2.07			1.67	
Punjab		0.00			2.82			2.82	
Rajasthan	4.62	4.42		4.62	4.42		3.87	3.62	
Sikkim		0.67			0.67			0.98	
Tamil Nadu	0.67			0.33		0.93		1.10	
Tripura		1.17		2.70	2.25		2.70	2.52	
Uttarakhand	1.50		6.67	2.87		6.67	2.47		2.67
Uttar Pradesh	3.57	1.50	4.17	3.57	1.50	4.17	4.32	1.20	1.67
West Bengal		1.98			1.98			2.39	2.34
Other		2.30			3.45			3.45	
Other	1.33		4.27	1.33		4.27	1.05		4.27

Source: SERCs 2010.
Note: APL = above poverty line; BPL = below poverty line; kWh = kilowatt-hour.
a. Kerala offers BPL customers free consumption only if they consume less than 18 kilowatt-hour per month.

Figure 3.4 Average Effective Tariffs for Urban Households in Rajasthan, 2010

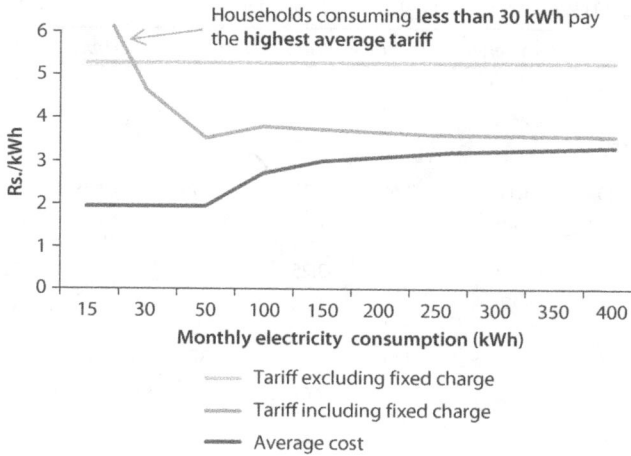

Sources: SERCs 2010; PFC 2011.

Uttarakhand, and Uttar Pradesh), the average low-consuming household pays more per kilowatt-hour than even the average household consuming more than 300 kilowatt-hour per month. In four states (Haryana, Kerala, Nagaland, and Punjab), this regressive tariff design is caused specifically by minimum charges, which are paid by 11–34 percent of households in those states, despite their low electricity-consumption levels.

Fixed charges can dramatically impact the average effective tariff. In Rajasthan, for example, an urban BPL or APL household pays an effective tariff of Rs. 5.95 per kilowatt-hour to consume 25 kilowatt-hour (figure 3.4). This rate, which is above the cost of supply, is much higher than the effective tariff at any higher consumption point. By contrast, a household that consumes 75 kilowatt-hour per month pays only Rs. 3.87 per kilowatt-hour, while a household consuming 300 kilowatt-hour a month pays even less (Rs. 3.60 per kilowatt-hour).

Concluding Remarks

This chapter has shown that the residential sector accounts for nearly a quarter of India's electricity consumption, suggesting that rationalizing electricity is critical for ensuring the financial viability of the distribution utilities and keeping subsidy costs low. Most states use similar tariff structures, but vary widely in their approaches to setting tariff levels and subsidy treatment. These differences, in turn, complicate the residential subsidy issue. But they also create opportunities for learning and applying best practices from Indian states and elsewhere to move toward better subsidy performance.

Annex 3A: State Tariff Schedules

State	Consumer group (and any consumption (kWh) restrictions)	Minimum payment (Rs.)	Fixed charge (Rs.) (and per load (KW) or consumption (kWh) as applicable)	Tariff (Rs.) per unit of consumption units of consumption to which tariff applies				
Andhra Pradesh	All	25	0	1.45 / 0–50	2.8 / 51–100	3.05 / 101–200	4.75 / 201–300	5.5 / 301+
Assam	< 5KW	0	30	3 / 0–120	4.05 / 121–240	4.75 / 241+		
	>= 5KW	0	30	4.35 / all				
	BPL, if <= 30 kWh/ month	0	15	2.35 / 0–30				
Bihar	All Urban / Rural with load > 2KW	40, <= 1KW; 40 + 20 per KW > 1KW	45, <= 3KW; 55, <= 4KW; 180, > 4KW	2.15 / 0–100	2.65 / 101–200	3.2 / 201–300	4 / 301+	
	Rural (load <=2KW), Metered	52, <= 1KW; 132.5, > 1KW	0	1.3 / 0–50	1.55 / 51–100	1.75 / 101+		
	Rural (load <=2KW), Unmetered	0	80, <= 1KW; 120, > 1KW	No variable rate				
	BPL, Urban, if <= 30 kWh/month	35	0					
	BPL, Rural, Metered, if <= 30 kWh/month	25	0					
	BPL, Rural, Unmetered, load < 1KW	0	35	No variable rate				
Chhattisgarh	All	30, <= 5KW; 100, > 5KW	0	1.6 / 0–200	1.9 / 0–500	2.45 / 0–700	3 / 0–701+	
	BPL, Metered, if <= 360 kWh in prev. year	0	0	1.5 / 0–30				
	BPL, Unmetered, <= 1KW	0	50	No variable rate				

table continues next page

Annex 3A: State Tariff Schedules *(continued)*

State	Consumer group (and any consumption (kWh) restrictions)	Minimum payment (Rs.)	Fixed charge (Rs.) (and per load (KW) or consumption (kWh) as applicable)	Tariff (Rs.) per unit of consumption units of consumption to which tariff applies				
Delhi	All	0	24, <= 2KW 60, <= 5KW 12 per KW, > 5KW	2.45 0–200	3.95 201–400	4.65 401+		
Goa	All	0	0	1.6 0–50	2.25 51–200	3 201–400	3.25 401+	
	BPL, if <= 30 kWh/month	0	24	0 0–30				
	Urban	0	5, <= 2KW 15, <= 4KW 30, <= 6KW 45, > 6KW	2.7 0–50	3 51–100	3.6 101–200	4.2 201–300	4.7 301+
Gujarat	Rural	0	5, <= 2KW 15, <= 4KW 30, <= 6KW 45, > 6KW	2.2 0–50	2.5 51–100	3.1 101–200	3.7 201–300	4.3 301+
	BPL	0	5	1.5 0–30				
Haryana	All	80	0	2.63 0–40	3.63 41–300	4.28 301+		
Himachal Pradesh	APL	0	25	0.7 0–150	1.7 151–300	2.45 301+		
	BPL	0	0	0.7 0–50				

table continues next page

State	Consumer group (and any consumption (kWh) restrictions)	Minimum payment (Rs.)	Fixed charge (Rs.) (and per load (KW) or consumption (kWh) as applicable)	Tariff (Rs.) per unit of consumption units of consumption to which tariff applies							
	All with load > 4 KW	0	40	1.7 / all							
	Urban, load <=4KW and Rural > 2KW	0	20	1.35 / 0–200	1.7 / 201+						
	Rural (load <=2KW), Metered	0	0	1 / all							
Jharkhand	Rural (load <=2KW), Unmetered	0	65	No variable rate							
	BPL, Metered, Load <= 0.1 KW	0	0	1 / all							
	BPL, Unmetered, Load <= 0.1 KW	0	27	No variable rate							
Karnataka	Urban	0	20, <= 1KW; 20 + 30 per KW, > 1KW	1.85 / 0–30	2.9 / 31–100	3.9 / 101–200	4.6 / 201–300	4.95 / 301–400	5.9 / 401+		
	Rural	0	10, <= 1KW; 10 + 20 per KW, > 1KW	1.85 / 0–30	2.9 / 31–100	3.7 / 101–200	4.3 / 201–300	4.65 / 301–400	5.2 / 401+		
	BPL, if <= 18 kWh/month	0	0	0 / 0–18							
Kerala	All	30, <= 5KW; 170, > 5KW	0	1.15 / 0–40	1.9 / 41–80	2.4 / 81–120	3 / 121–150	3.65 / 151–200	4.3 / 201–300	5.3 / 301–500	5.45 / 501+
	BPL, load <= 0.5 KW, if <= 20 kWh/month	0	0	0 / 0–20							

table continues next page

Annex 3A: State Tariff Schedules *(continued)*

State	Consumer group (and any consumption (kWh) restrictions)	Minimum payment (Rs.)	Fixed charge (Rs.) (and per load (KW) or consumption (kWh) as applicable)	Tariff (Rs.) per unit of consumption / units of consumption to which tariff applies
Madhya Pradesh	Urban, Metered	30	10, <= 50 kWh 20, <= 100 kWh 40 per 0.5KW, <= 200 kWh 45 per 0.5KW, > 200 kWh	2.9 (0–50); 3.3 (51–100); 3.9 (101–200); 4 (201+)
	Urban, Unmetered	0	255	No variable rate
	Rural, Metered	30	5, <= 50 kWh 10, <= 100 kWh 20 per 0.5KW, <= 200 kWh 30 per 0.5KW, > 200 kWh	2.9 (0–50); 3.3 (51–100); 3.9 (101–200); 4 (201+)
	Rural, Unmetered	0	84.5	No variable rate
	All with <= 30 kWh/month	30	0	2.65 (0–30)
Maharashtra	All	0	30, <= 5KW 100, > 5KW	2.35 (0–100); 4.25 (101–300); 5.85 (301–500); 6.85 (501+)
	BPL, if <= 30 kWh/month	0	3	0.66 (all)
Manipur	Metered	0	60 per KW	2.2 (0–100); 2.7 (101–200); 3.2 (201+)
	Unmetered	0	220 + 60 per KW	No variable rate
	BPL, Metered, if <= 15 kWh/month	0	20	1 (0–15)
	BPL, Unmetered	0	35	No variable rate

table continues next page

Annex 3A: State Tariff Schedules *(continued)*

State	Consumer group (and any consumption (kWh) restrictions)	Minimum payment (Rs.)	Fixed charge (Rs.) (and per load (KW) or consumption (kWh) as applicable)	Tariff (Rs.) per unit of consumption / units of consumption to which tariff applies				
Meghalaya	All	0	25	2.25 / 0–100	2.65 / 101–200	3.65 / 201+		
	BPL, if <= 30 kWh/ month	0	0	0 / 0–30				
Mizoram	Metered	0	25 per KW	1.5 / 0–50	1.85 / 51–100	2.5 / 101–200	3.5 / 201+	
	Unmetered	0	75 + 25 per KW	No variable rate				
	BPL, Metered, if <= 15 kWh/month	0	10	0.9 / 0–15				
	BPL, Unmetered	0	23.5	No variable rate				
Nagaland	All	70 per KW	0	2.3 / 0–30	2.9 / 31–100	3.2 / 101–250	3.5 / 251+	
Orissa	All	0	20, <= 1KW; 20 + 10 per KW, > 1 KW	1.4 / 0–100	2.3 / 101–200	3.1 / 201+		
	BPL	0	30	0 / 0–30				
Punjab	All	35 per KW	0	2.82 / 0–100	4.28 / 101–300	4.52 / 301+		
	BPL, load <= 1 KW	0	0	0 / 0–200				
Rajasthan	Urban	0	80, <= 50 kWh; 105, > 50 kWh	1.95 / 0–50	3.5 / 51+			
	Rural	0	80, <= 50 kWh; 105, > 50 kWh	1.755 / 0–50	3.15 / 51+			
Sikkim	All	20, <= 5KW; 170, > 5KW	0	0.6 / 0–50	1.75 / 51–100	3.15 / 101–200	3.75 / 201–400	4 / 401+

table continues next page

Annex 3A: State Tariff Schedules *(continued)*

State	Consumer group (and any consumption (kWh) restrictions)	Minimum payment (Rs.)	Fixed charge (Rs.) (and per load (KW) or consumption (kWh) as applicable)	Tariff (Rs.) per unit of consumption units of consumption to which tariff applies				
Tamil Nadu	All	20	5	0.75 *0–25*	0.85 *26–50*	1.5 *51–100*	2.2 *101–300*	3.05 *301+*
	All with if <= 50 kWh/month	20	0	0.65 *0–25*	0.75 *26–50*			
	BPL, rural	0	10	No variable rate				
Tripura	3-phase connection	0	40 per KW	4.65 *all*				
	Urban, single-phase	0	15, <= 50 kWh; 25, <= 150 kWh; 30, > 150 kWh	2.2 *0–50*	3.1 *51–150*	3.9 *151–300*	4.7 *301+*	
	Rural, single-phase	0	10, <= 30 kWh; 15, <= 50 kWh; 25, <= 150 kWh; 30, > 150 kWh	1.92 *0–30*	2.2 *31–50*	3.1 *51–150*	3.9 *151–300*	4.7 *301+*
	BPL	0	35	No variable rate				
Uttarakhand	All Urban and Rural Metered	0	20, <= 4KW; 40, > 4KW	2.2 *all*				
	Rural, Unmetered	0	200	No variable rate				
	BPL, load <= 1KW, if <= 30 kWh/month	0	0	1.5 *0–30*				
Uttar Pradesh	Urban	0	65 per KW	3.45 *0–200*	3.8 *201+*			
	Urban with <= 150 kWh/month	0	50	1.9 *0–100*	2.5 *101–150*			
	Rural, Metered	0	15 per KW	1 *all*				
	Rural, Unmetered	0	125	No variable rate				

table continues next page

28

State	Consumer group (and any consumption (kWh) restrictions)	Minimum payment (Rs.)	Fixed charge (Rs.) (and per load (KW) or consumption (kWh) as applicable)	Tariff (Rs.) per unit of consumption units of consumption to which tariff applies					
	Urban	0	5 per KW	2.32 / 0–75	2.61 / 76–150	3.1 / 151–300	3.62 / 301–450	3.82 / 451–900	5.96 / 901+
	Rural	0	5 per KW	2.27 / 0–75	2.51 / 76–180	3.05 / 181–300	3.55 / 301–600	3.65 / 601–900	5.96 / 901+
West Bengal	All with <= 75 kWh/ month	0	2.5	1.9 / 0–75					
	BPL, if <= 25 kWh/ month	0	0	0 / 0–25					
	Single-phase connection	28	0	3.45 / all					
Other	3-phase connection	46	0	3.45 / all					
	BPL	46	0	2.3 / all					
	Metered	0, <= 1/4KW 25 <= 1/2 KW 40, <= 1KW 10 per 0.25 KW > 1KW	0	0.9 / 0–30	1.15 / 31–100	1.4 / 101–200	2.1 / 201+		
Other	Unmetered	15	50, <= 1/4KW 160, <= 1/2KW 240, <= 3/4KW 320, <= 1KW 635, <= 2KW 635 + 275 per 0.5KW, > 2KW	No variable rate					

Source: SERCs 2010.

Note: State tariff schedules are for fiscal year 2009/10, except in the cases of Goa, Manipur, and Mizoram, for which 2010/11 schedules are used (earlier schedules were unavailable). APL = above poverty line; BPL = below poverty line; KW = kilowatt; kWh = kilowatt-hour.

Notes

1. India's central government sets the overarching policies for the power sector, while the states implement these policies and pay the subsidies.
2. All states charge a tariff per kilowatt-hour of electricity consumption, with the exception of schedules for unmetered consumers and some states' schedules for BPL customers; in these cases, all consumers are charged the same fixed amount.
3. This consumption level aligns with the Government of India's vision to provide all households a minimum subsistence level of at least 30 kilowatt-hour per month.
4. This electricity consumption level is the India-wide average for households in 2010, based on National Sample Survey data.

CHAPTER 4

Subsidy Size and Household Distribution

An overwhelming majority of states in India subsidize a substantial portion of their residential electricity consumption. Given that the residential sector consumes about one-quarter of all electricity sold in India, subsidized residential electricity accounts for a large portion of total electricity consumption. This chapter examines the prevalence and magnitude of residential subsidies across states and their distribution across households. The next section considers the gap between supply costs and tariffs.

Average Supply Cost and Tariffs

The size of states' subsidies is determined, in part, by the average cost of electricity supply. For most states, the average supply cost is higher than the average effective tariff. At one end of the spectrum, two states (including Sikkim) have average effective tariffs that are slightly higher than the average cost of supply. Utilities in some states (for example, Maharashtra, Orissa, and Punjab) lose relatively small amounts per unit of energy. At the other extreme, utilities in several states (Himachal Pradesh, Mizoram, and Tamil Nadu) lose nearly Rs. 4 on every unit of electricity supplied to households. Figure 4.1 shows that the average supply cost ranges from Rs. 1.3 per kilowatt-hour in Sikkim to more than four times that amount (Rs. 6.2 per kilowatt-hour) in Mizoram, with an overall average of Rs. 3.8. Appendix C provides state-level data on the average supply cost and average effective tariffs paid by households across all electricity consumption.

Subsidy Prevalence and Magnitude

Electricity subsidies in India are both prevalent and large. In the majority of tariff schedules, most electricity units are subsidized (that is, priced below average cost), while only some are cross-subsidized (that is, priced above average cost).

Figure 4.1 Average Supply Costs and Average Effective Tariffs for States, by Subsidy Size, 2010

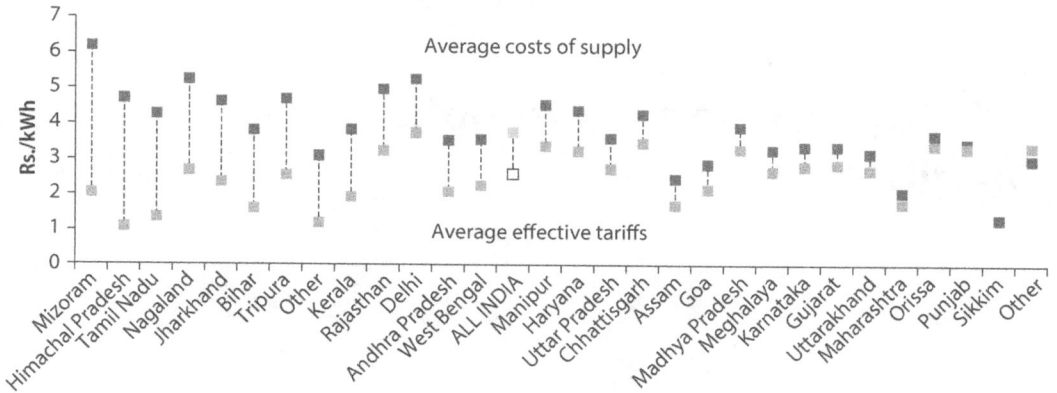

Sources: National Sample Survey 2010; PFC 2011; SERCs 2010.

The percent of electricity units priced below cost indicates subsidy prevalence. The difference between cost and tariff on those subsidized units indicates the magnitude of subsidies, while the difference between tariff and cost on the cross-subsidized units indicates the magnitude of cross-subsidies. Together, prevalence and magnitude define a state's subsidy regime and indicate whether the state is paying a net subsidy or receiving a net cross-subsidy over all electricity consumption. Figure 4.1 shows that nearly all states are paying net subsidies, meaning they set average effective tariffs over all units of subsidized and cross-subsidized consumption below cost.

An overwhelming 87 percent of all residential electricity consumption is subsidized—equivalent to 21 percent of all electricity consumed in India (2010 figure). Nineteen states subsidize more electricity than the all-India average. In seven states (including Assam, Delhi, Himachal Pradesh, Nagaland, Tamil Nadu, and Tripura), virtually all residential consumption is sold at tariffs below cost recovery. For any of these states to recover their supply costs, the magnitude of cross-subsidies on the small number of cross-subsidized units would have to be substantially larger than the magnitude of subsidies on the subsidized units. Among the best performers is Punjab, which subsidizes only 59 percent of total residential consumption (figure 4.2).

For the 87 percent of subsidized, residential electricity consumption, the average subsidy is Rs. 1.5 per kilowatt-hour. The average cost of electricity supply is Rs. 3.78 per kilowatt-hour. By contrast, for the 13 percent of cross-subsidized consumption, the average cross-subsidy is just Rs. 0.62 per kilowatt-hour (figure 4.3). In nearly all states, the average subsidy is larger than the average cross-subsidy. Mizoram provides the starkest example, with an average subsidy of Rs. 3.5 per kilowatt-hour for subsidized units and no cross-subsidized units. Just three states have average cross-subsidies that are larger than average subsidies

Figure 4.2 Prevalence of State Subsidies, 2010

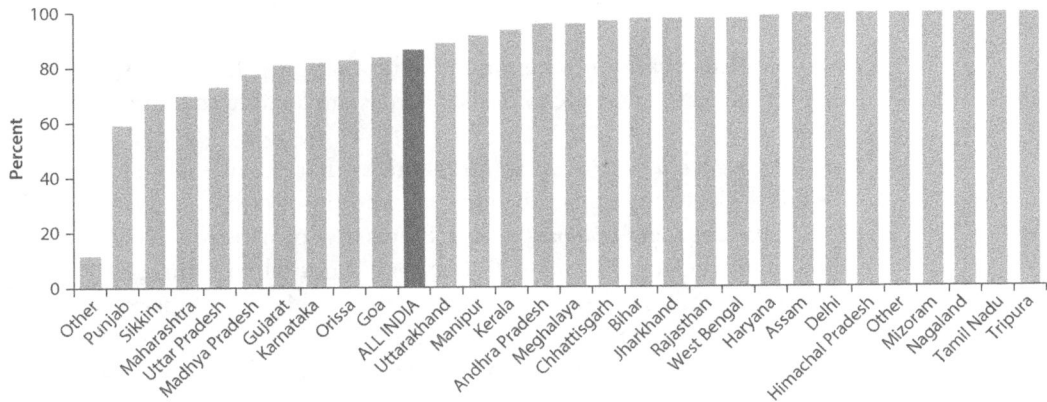

Sources: National Sample Survey 2010; PFC 2011; SERCs 2010.

Figure 4.3 Magnitude of State Subsidies and Cross-Subsides, 2010

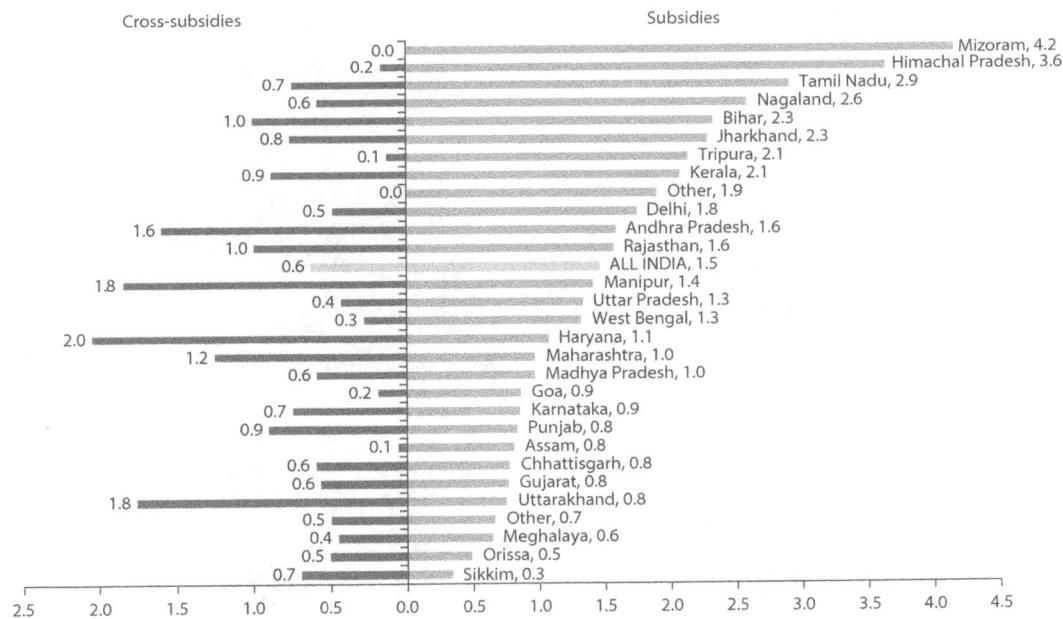

Sources: National Sample Survey 2010; PFC 2011; SERCs 2010.

(Haryana, Manipur, and Uttarakhand). In these states, the share of units charged at a cross-subsidy is too low to recover costs, even with the higher average cross-subsidy. Appendix D provides state-level data on average subsidies and cross-subsidies.

Combining prevalence and magnitude (as a percent of cost) allows us to divide states into four categories (figure 4.4):

1. *Low prevalence and low magnitude.* States that provide relatively small subsidies on only a few electricity units. There is only one state that falls into this group.
2. *Low prevalence and high magnitude.* States that provide large subsidies on only a few electricity units. No states fall into this group.
3. *High prevalence and low magnitude.* States that provide relatively small subsidies on most electricity units. Twenty-one states fall into this group including Andhra Pradesh, Assam, Chhattisgarh, Delhi, Goa, Gujarat, Haryana, Karnataka, Madhya Pradesh, Maharashtra, Manipur, Meghalaya, Nagaland, Orissa, Punjab, Rajasthan, Sikkim, Tripura, Uttarakhand, Uttar Pradesh, and West Bengal.
4. *High prevalence and high magnitude.* States that provide large subsidies on most electricity units. Seven states fall into this group including Bihar, Himachal Pradesh, Jharkhand, Kerala, Mizoram, and Tamil Nadu.

Figure 4.4 State Subsidy Groupings, by Prevalence and Magnitude, 2010

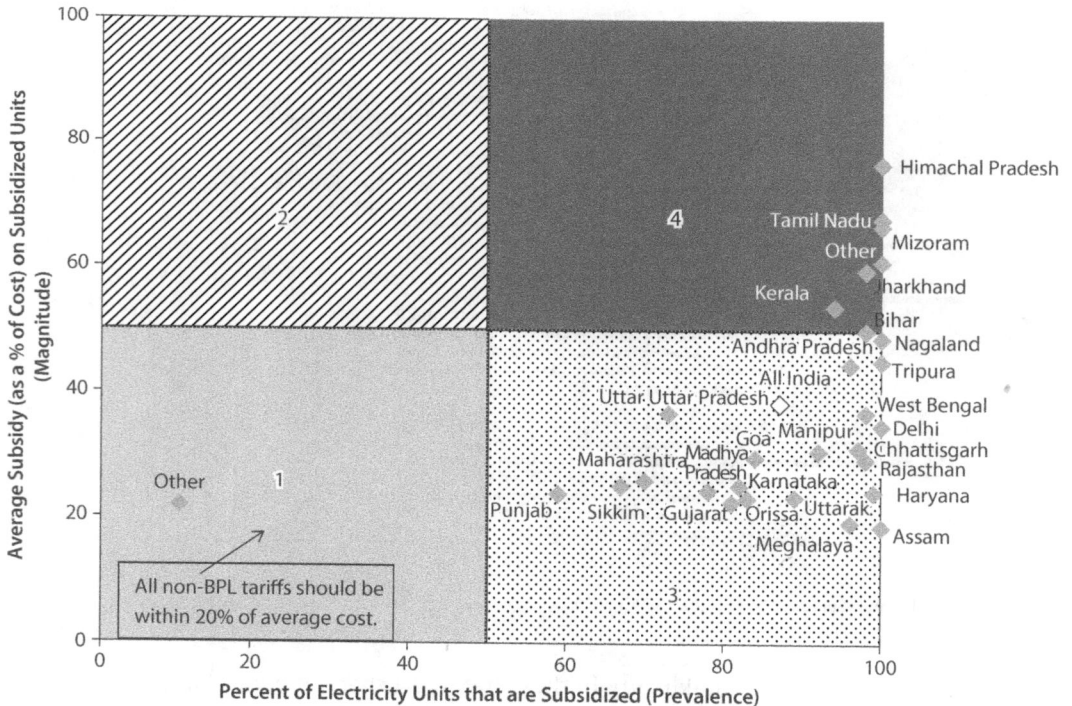

Sources: National Sample Survey 2010; PFC 2011; SERCs 2010.

The quadrants shown in figure 4.4, by definition, refer to high and low group-ings using the 50 percent mark for prevalence and magnitude. However, the Government of India's directive mandated that states were to have achieved a much lower level of cross-subsidization by 2011. All tariffs were to have been set within 20 percent above or below the cost of supply. The only exceptions were below the poverty line (BPL) and other low-consumption customers, in which cases, tariffs were to have been set below a minimum threshold decided by the states (suggested at 30 kilowatt-hour per month) and subsidized by no more than 50 percent. At present, no state is meeting this directive on an individual tariff basis, and only one (Assam) has an average subsidy below 20 percent of cost.

Distribution of Subsidies and Cross-Subsidies

Of the three-quarters of households with electricity access in 2010, 7 percent cross-subsidized the 93 percent that were subsidized. An overwhelming 86 per-cent of customers paid no cross-subsidy, meaning they received subsidies on all of their electricity consumption; 7 percent paid an average tariff below cost, mean-ing they received more in subsidy than they paid in cross-subsidy. About 2 percent paid a net cross-subsidy, meaning they paid more in subsidy than they received in cross-subsidy, while 5 percent paid full cost, receiving no subsidy (figure 4.5).

Figure 4.5 suggests that households might be divided into four broad group-ings according to how much subsidy they receive. One group receives a subsidy on every electricity unit it consumes. A second group receives some subsidies and pays some cross-subsidies, but is net-subsidized overall. A third group receives some subsidies and pays some cross-subsidies, but is net cross-subsidized overall. Finally, a fourth group receives no subsidy on any of its electricity consumption. Figure 4.6 shows how a typical tariff schedule with an increasing block tariff (IBT) structure and a fixed cost divides households into these four subsidy and cross-subsidy groupings.

Figure 4.5 Household Subsidy Coverage, 2010

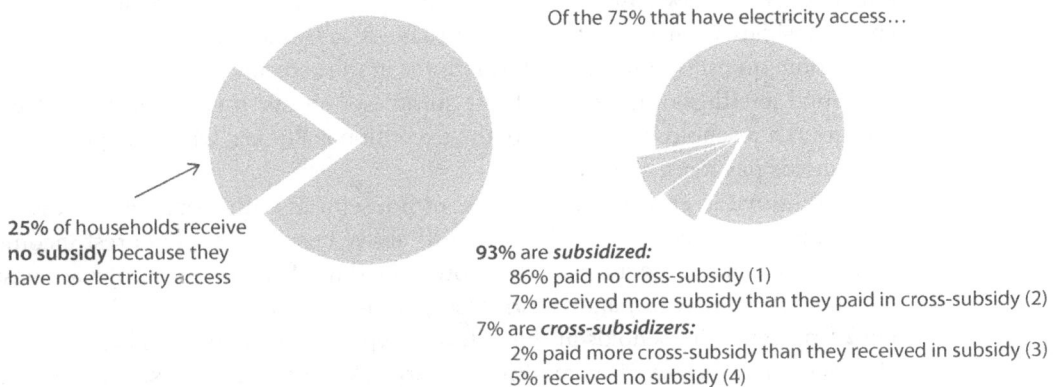

Of the 75% that have electricity access...

25% of households receive **no subsidy** because they have no electricity access

93% are *subsidized*:
   86% paid no cross-subsidy (1)
   7% received more subsidy than they paid in cross-subsidy (2)
7% are ***cross-subsidizers*:**
   2% paid more cross-subsidy than they received in subsidy (3)
   5% received no subsidy (4)

Sources: National Sample Survey 2010; PFC 2011; SERCs 2010.

Figure 4.6 Average Effective Tariffs and Subsidies with IBT Structure, 2010

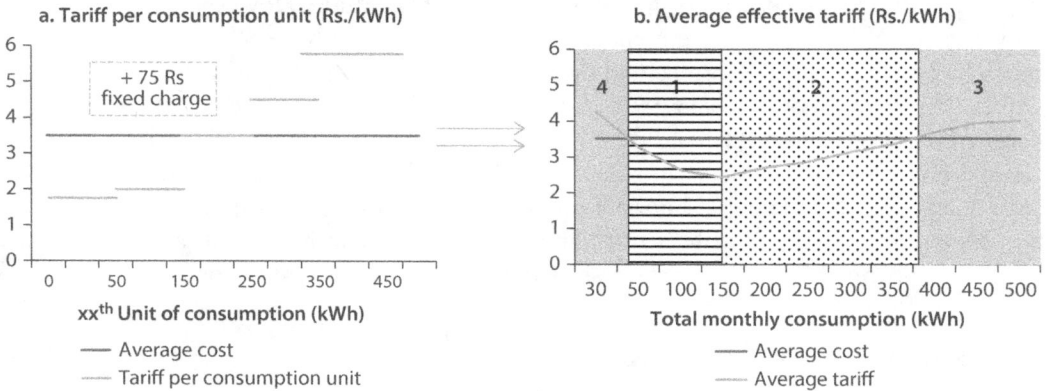

Source: World bank.

1. *Full subsidy group.* For the 86 percent of households that have electricity, consumption is billed at an effective tariff below cost. Twenty-two percent of the households in this group belong to the poorest income quintile, while the other 78 percent are spread relatively evenly across the other four income quintiles. Notably, 17 percent of households that belong to the richest income quintile are in this group (figure 4.7). In the vast majority of states, more than half of house-holds—and nearly 100 percent in some cases—fall into the full subsidy group; among the two exceptions is Sikkim (figure 4.8).

2. *Net subsidy group.* Seven percent of all households with electricity access receive a subsidy on average, paying below cost for their initial consumption and above cost for the remainder. Three-quarters of this group are found in the two richest income quintiles, while 15 percent are in the two poorest quintiles. In seven states (Goa, Gujarat, Karnataka, Maharashtra, Orissa, Punjab, and Sikkim), this category accounts for one-fifth to one-quarter of households with electricity. For all other states, the numbers of households in this category are few to none.

3. *Net cross-subsidy group.* This group comprises 2 percent of households with electricity access. For these households, initial consumption is billed at an effective tariff below cost and the remainder above cost; but on average, they pay cross-subsidies. Nearly two-thirds of households in this group belong to the rich-est income quintile, while another quarter is in the second-richest quintile. None are found in either of the two poorest quintiles. The vast majority of states have few or no households in this group; the exception is Punjab, where 21 percent of households pay a net cross-subsidy.

4. *No subsidy group.* For 5 percent of households with electricity access, all consumption is billed at an effective tariff above cost. The two poorest income quintiles comprise 38 percent of this group. The third and fourth quintiles account for another 38 percent, and the richest income quintile makes up the remain-ing 25 percent. Households in this category typically consume small amounts of electricity and pay fixed or minimum charges. Other households in this group

Figure 4.7 Distribution of Subsidy Groups, by Income Quintile, 2010

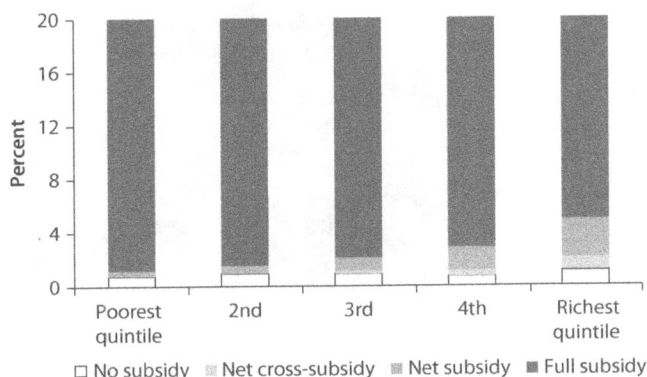

Sources: National Sample Survey 2010; PFC 2011; SERCs 2010.

Figure 4.8 Distribution of Subsidy Groups, by State, 2010

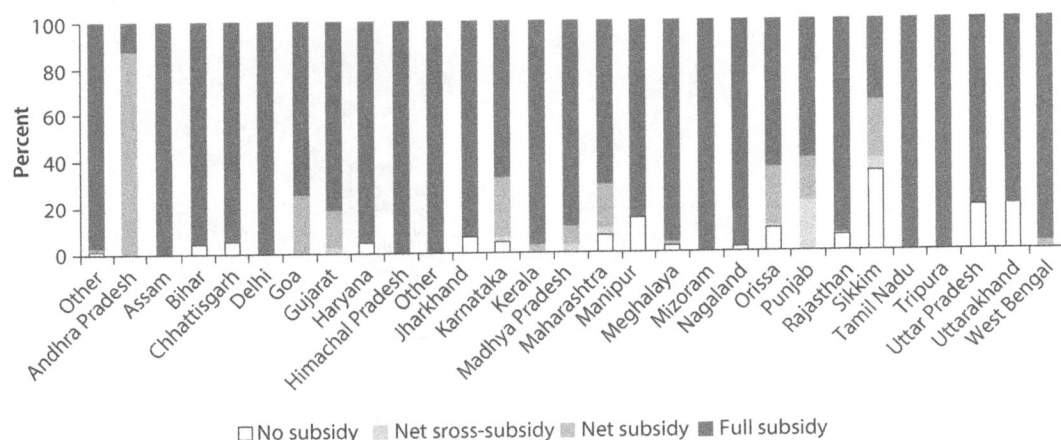

Sources: National Sample Survey 2010; PFC 2011; SERCs 2010.

may include those in a high-consumption block of a volume-differentiated tariff (VDT) (for example, Chhattisgarh), where they are charged the same above-cost tariff on all consumption, or those who pay according to an IBT schedule that bills all consumption blocks above cost. States with a large percentage of households in the no subsidy group include Sikkim (34 percent), Uttarakhand (20 percent), Uttar Pradesh (19 percent), and Manipur (15 percent).

An average household that receives a subsidy on at least one unit of electricity (that is, any household in group 1, 2, or 3) receives a total monthly subsidy of Rs. 105 on average (figure 4.9a). With the subsidy, the average household pays a monthly electricity bill of Rs. 206. The subsidy amount varies somewhat by income group: the poorest quintile receives an average monthly subsidy of Rs. 88 and pays a monthly bill of Rs. 109, while the richest one receives Rs. 136

Figure 4.9 Average Household Subsidy and Cross-Subsidy, by Income Quintile, 2010

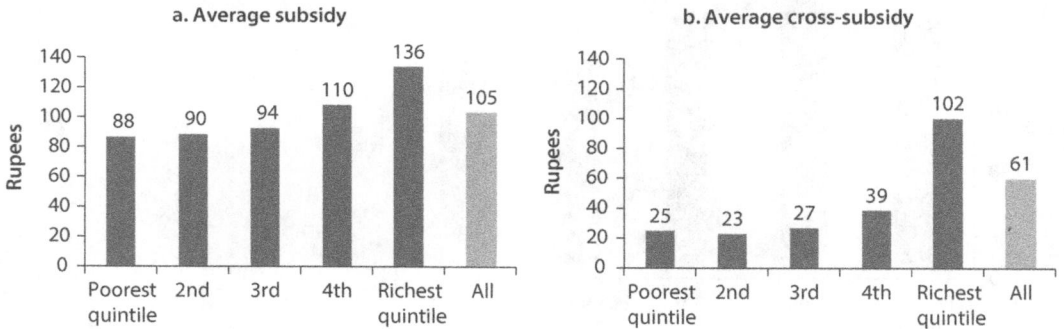

a. Average subsidy

b. Average cross-subsidy

Sources: National Sample Survey 2010; PFC 2011; SERCs 2010.

Figure 4.10 Average Household Subsidy, by State, 2010

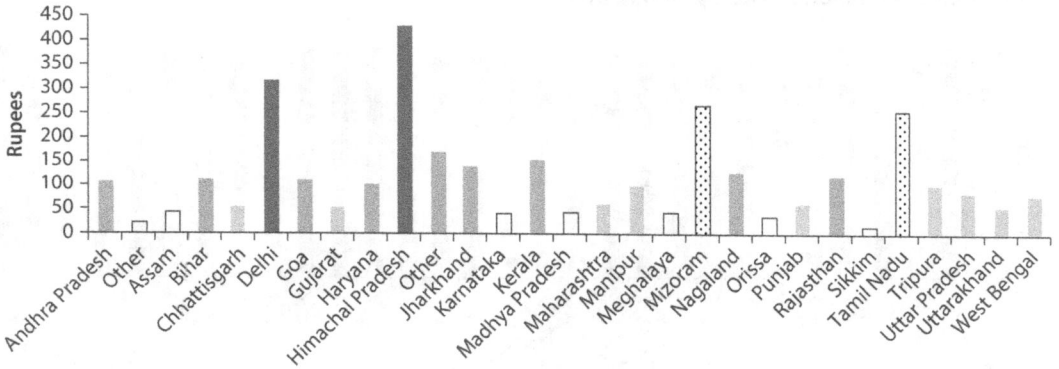

Sources: National Sample Survey 2010; PFC 2011; SERCs 2010.

a month in average subsidy and pays Rs. 357. By contrast, the average household that pays a cross-subsidy on at least one unit of electricity (that is, households in groups 2, 3, and 4) pays a total monthly cross-subsidy of Rs. 61. This amount varies somewhat by income group, with the poorest quintile paying a monthly average of Rs. 25, and the richest one paying an average of Rs. 102 a month (figure 4.9b). Average household subsidies vary widely by state, ranging from lows of Rs. 15 in Sikkim to respective highs of Rs. 318 and Rs. 429 in Delhi and Himachal Pradesh (figure 4.10). Appendix E provides state-level data on subsidy distribution by household group and average household subsidy and cross-subsidy.

Concluding Remarks

This chapter has shown that, in most states, all households are eligible for a subsidy on at least a portion of their monthly electricity consumption. In addition, households in the poorest two income quintiles consume significantly less electricity

than those in the upper income quintiles. Together, these two factors mean that
wealthier households with electricity access are typically eligible for just as much,
if not more, subsidy as poorer households with electricity. Furthermore, the poorest income quintiles comprise the largest portion of the 25 percent of households
that remain without electricity in India. This means a relatively larger share of
poorer households is unable to take advantage of tariff subsidies. Finally, cross-
subsidy payments are limited. The next chapter takes a closer look at the issue of
subsidy leakage to the non-poor and the barriers to better targeting of the poor.

CHAPTER 5

Targeting of Subsidies

This chapter analyzes India's subsidy distribution by household income, focusing particularly on the share that reaches below the poverty line (BPL) households. The first section compares state-level subsidy payments, including the impact of cross-subsidies. The second section identifies the major factors that skew subsidy leakage to the higher-income groups and impede better targeting of the poor.

Subsidy Incidence

This analysis finds that more than half of India's total subsidy payments are received by households in the top two-fifths of the income ladder (figure 5.1). In 2010, the first and second income quintiles accounted for just 14 percent and 16 percent, respectively, of subsidy payments. Furthermore, these estimates are conservative because they assume that BPL and above the poverty line (APL) households are accurately identified (box 5.1). Figure 5.1 shows the slight improvement in distribution resulting from cross-subsidy payments. Even so, there is 45 percent leakage to the top two income quintiles.[1]

State comparisons show that the weakest subsidy targeting is found in Assam, Jharkhand, Sikkim, and Uttar Pradesh, followed by Bihar, a large state with a substantial BPL population (figure 5.2). In Assam, where 72 percent of subsidies leak to the richest two income quintiles, the poorest quintile receives just 6 percent of all subsidy payments. In Uttar Pradesh and Bihar, most subsidy payments are received by the top two income quintiles, at 61 percent and 62 percent, respectively (table F.1, appendix F).

Cross-subsidy payments reduce leakage to the upper quintiles somewhat (for example, 20 states report less subsidy leakage with cross-subsidies). But the reduction is small, averaging 6 percent to the fifth income quintile and 2 percent to the fourth. The greatest impact from cross-subsidy payments is found in Punjab and Maharashtra. In both states, the richest quintile pays a net cross-subsidy; in the case of Punjab, the fourth quintile also pays more in cross-subsidy than it receives in subsidy (figure 5.3).

Figure 5.1 Subsidy Incidence across India, 2010

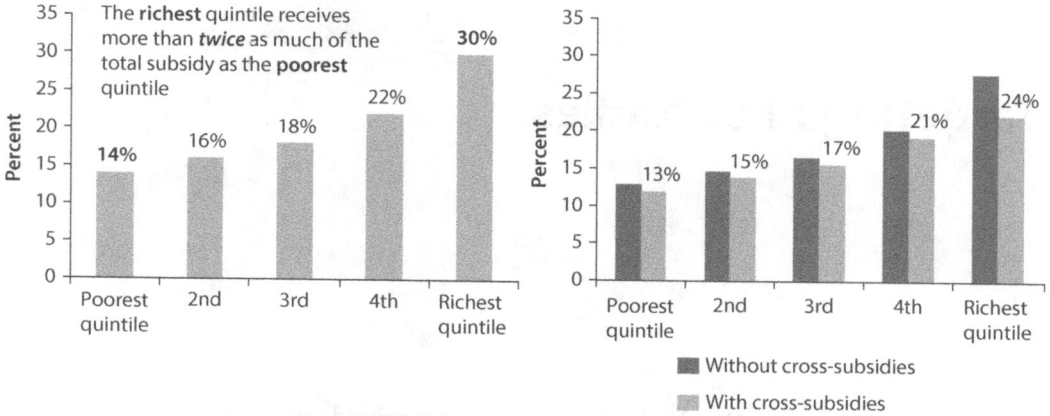

The **richest** quintile receives more than *twice* as much of the total subsidy as the **poorest** quintile

Left chart:
- Poorest quintile: 14%
- 2nd: 16%
- 3rd: 18%
- 4th: 22%
- Richest quintile: 30%

Right chart:
- Poorest quintile: 13%
- 2nd: 15%
- 3rd: 17%
- 4th: 21%
- Richest quintile: 24%

■ Without cross-subsidies
▩ With cross-subsidies

Sources: National Sample Survey 2010; PFC 2011; SERCs 2010.

Box 5.1 Baseline Assumption: Accurate BPL Household Identification

A critical assumption underlying this study's findings is that only BPL households receive the BPL or Kutir Jyoti tariff, if specified. In reality, however, errors are likely if states cannot accurately identify BPL households. This means some APL households may be included as BPL households and that a proportion of BPL households may be excluded. Most BPL benefits are delivered to BPL cardholders, which are given to households identified as poor in the government-run BPL census. But recent studies suggest that up to two-fifths BPL cardholders are non-poor households, and more than half of poor households do not have BPL cards (Ram, Mohanty, and Ram 2009; Mahamallik and Sahu 2011).

Because BPL tariffs are lower than APL tariffs, this study's assumption that BPL tariffs are applied only to all BPL households with electricity could lead to overestimating the subsidies delivered to the lower quintiles and underestimating subsidy leakage to the higher quintiles. Despite this limitation, the findings demonstrate high percentages of subsidies going to APL households (figure B5.1.1). Thus, the baseline assumption can be taken as a conservative estimate of India's residential subsidy leakage.

Assuming that BPL cards are misallocated, as researchers have found, worsens the estimated subsidy incidence and BPL targeting.[a] Misallocating BPL cards reduces the per-unit subsidy that some BPL households receive by treating them as APL households. Conversely, it increases the per-unit subsidy that some APL households receive by treating them as BPL households. The total subsidy receipts for BPL households are changed only slightly since they consume relatively little electricity. But those of APL households, who consume more electricity, increase significantly. As a result, subsidy incidence is further skewed toward the upper quintiles.

Source: World Bank.

box continues next page

Box 5.1   Baseline Assumption: Accurate BPL Household Identification *(continued)*

Figure B5.1.1   Subsidy Incidence under BPL Misidentification, 2010

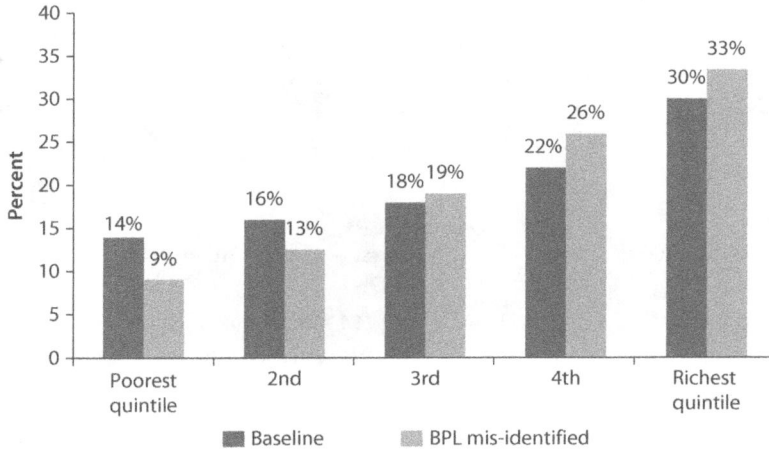

Source: World Bank

a. To model researchers' findings, we simulated the misallocation of BPL cards by categorizing 40 percent of randomly selected BPL households as APL households and categorizing the same number of randomly selected APL households as BPL households. The results roughly approximate the magnitude of the impact of inaccurate BPL identification.

Figure 5.2   Subsidy Incidence in Selected States, 2010

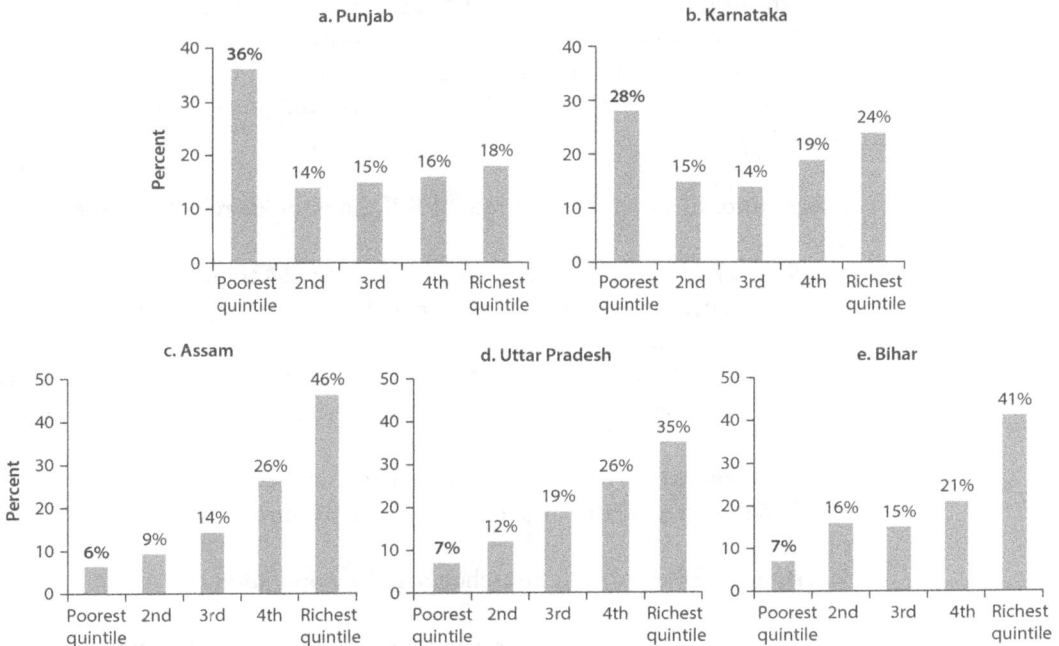

Sources: National Sample Survey 2010; PFC 2011; SERCs 2010.

Figure 5.3 Impact of Cross-Subsidies on Subsidy Incidence, 2010

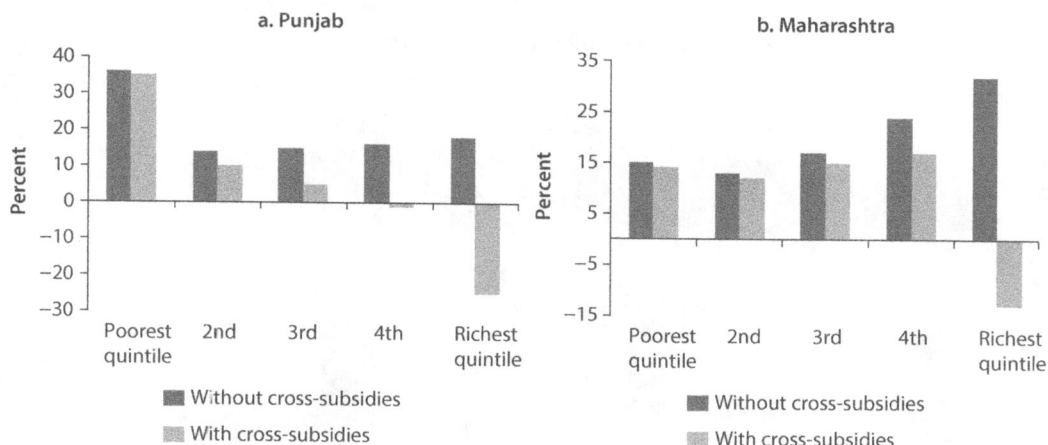

Sources: National Sample Survey 2010; PFC 2011; SERCs 2010.

What Prevents Better Subsidy Targeting?

Only 13 percent of the subsidies paid by India's states reach BPL households. For 11 states, the figure is below 10 percent (figure 5.4. The other 87 percent is delivered to APL HHs. For 15 states, the reported BPL targeting is worse than the all-India average. Five states perform better than the average but still report less than 20 percent BPL targeting. Only one state performs by far the best, with 100 percent BPL targeting. Manipur is the second-best performer, at 43 percent, followed by Punjab and Karnataka, with 33 percent each.

Five factors determine the share of subsidies delivered to any population segment (Komives et al. 2005). Applied to BPL households, these factors are defined as follows:

1. *Access ratio.* Electricity access rate of BPL households relative to the overall access rate;[2]
2. *Beneficiary ratio.* Share of BPL households with electricity that benefit from subsidies relative to the share of total beneficiaries among the entire population with electricity;
3. *Subsidy ratio.* Average rate of subsidization across all electricity consumed by BPL household beneficiaries relative to the average subsidy rate for all beneficiaries;
4. *Consumption ratio.* Average quantity of electricity consumed by BPL household beneficiaries relative to the average consumption by all beneficiaries; and
5. *Poverty rate.* Share of BPL households in the population.

This disaggregation shows that several types of factors explain why subsidies do not reach BPL households: (i) access, (ii) tariff design, and (iii) poverty rate.

Figure 5.4 Percent of Subsidies Received by BPL Households, 2010

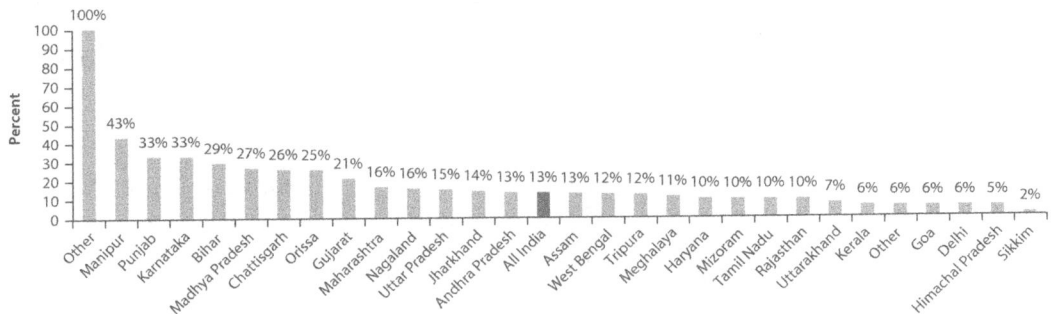

Sources: National Sample Survey 2010; PFC 2011; SERCs 2010.

Access factors are measured by the access ratio. Tariff-design factors are measured by the product of the beneficiary, subsidy, and consumption ratios, which indicates the ratio of the average subsidy received by a BPL household with electricity to the average subsidy received by any household with electricity.[3] Poverty rate, unlike access and tariff design, is an uncontrollable factor, meaning it is not easily influenced by states' electricity policy choices.

Figure 5.5 shows India's overall score on access and tariff-design factors, along with the poverty rate. The product of these three scores, 0.13, is the all-India BPL targeting rate. The access score, 0.72, reflects the fact that the BPL access rate, 53 percent, is only three-quarters that of the total population. The tariff design score, 0.75, reflects the fact that the average BPL household with electricity receives three-quarters the size of the subsidy that the average household with electricity (BPL or APL) receives; that is, the intended subsidy recipients, BPL households, are getting less of a subsidy than the unintended recipients (table F.2, appendix F).

Comparing India's scores on access and tariff design to the maximum extent possible suggests significantly more room for improving tariff design, at least in terms of the subsidy targeting goal. The maximum possible access score is 1.00, which occurs when the electricity access rate of BPL households is equal to the overall access rate.[4] By contrast, the maximum possible tariff-design score is 5.72, which is the inverse of the poverty rate multiplied by the inverse of the access score. This occurs when there is perfect subsidy targeting to BPL households (that is, all subsidies reach BPL households, without any leakage to APL households).

Disaggregating the tariff-design score into the beneficiary, subsidy, and consumption ratios can reveal what is driving the low score (figure 5.6). The beneficiary ratio is 1.01, indicating that the share of BPL households receiving a subsidy is nearly equal to the share of APL households receiving a subsidy. The subsidy ratio is 1.25, indicating that the average BPL beneficiary receives a greater per-unit discount on electricity than does the average APL beneficiary. Finally, the consumption ratio is 0.59, indicating that the APL beneficiary's average electricity consumption is significantly higher than the average consumption of a BPL beneficiary.

Elite Capture • http://dx.doi.org/10.1596/978-1-4648-0412-0

Figure 5.5 Disaggregation of BPL Subsidy Targeting, 2010

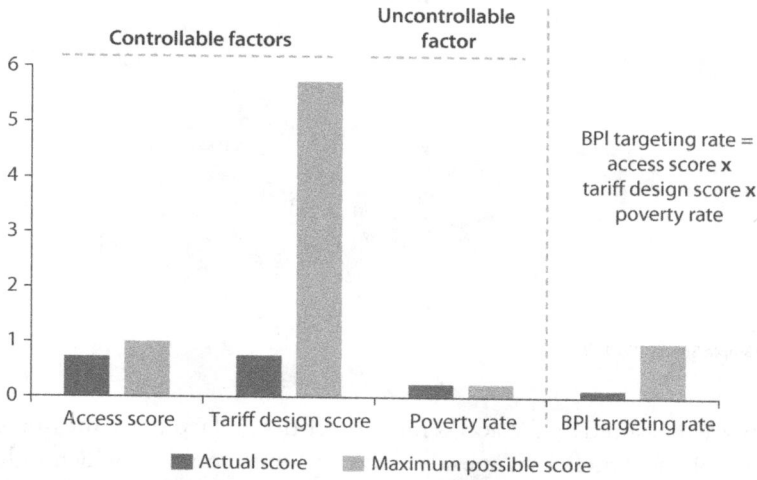

Sources: National Sample Survey 2010; PFC 2011; SERCs 2010.
Note: The poverty rate is assumed to be fixed since it is not easily influenced by electricity policy choices.
BPL = below poverty line.

Figure 5.6 Disaggregation of Tariff Design Score, 2010

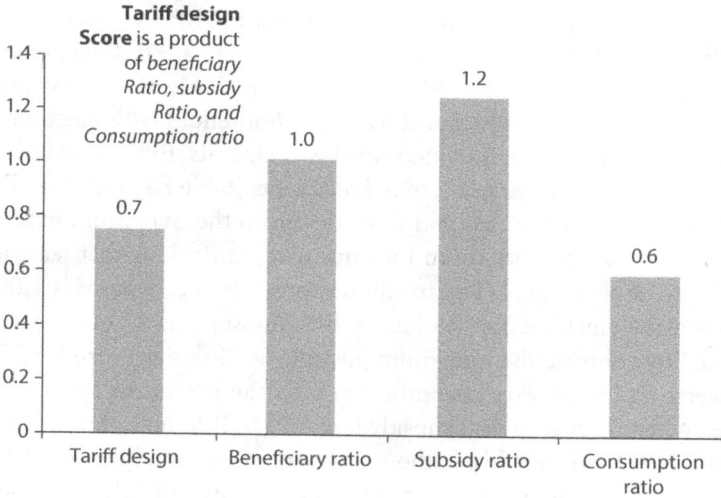

Sources: National Sample Survey 2010; PFC 2011; SERCs 2010.

The disaggregation suggests room for improvement in all three areas. The beneficiary ratio would increase significantly if states reduced the number of APL households receiving a subsidy. In terms of the subsidy ratio, the vast majority of households currently receive a subsidy. BPL beneficiaries receive a greater per-unit discount than APL households, but states could shift even more subsidies to BPL households by increasing that differential. States have less control over the consumption ratio; however, lowering BPL tariffs and/or increasing APL tariffs would induce increased BPL electricity consumption and decreased APL consumption, which would shift subsidies toward BPL households.

Most states echo the all-India pattern, having significantly more room to improve their tariff design than electricity access. In most states, the beneficiary ratio is slightly higher than 1.0, the subsidy ratio is somewhat greater than 1.0, and the consumption ratio is well under 1.0. In terms of the beneficiary ratio, nine states give subsidies to a greater share of APL households than BPL households (Andhra Pradesh, Haryana, Jharkhand, Nagaland, Punjab, Rajasthan, Sikkim, Uttarakhand, and Uttar Pradesh). For the subsidy ratio, six states are exceptions (Jharkhand, Mizoram, Nagaland, Rajasthan, Sikkim, and Uttar Pradesh), meaning that they give APL households a greater per-unit discount than BPL households (table F.3, appendix F).

Concluding Remarks

This analysis finds that an overwhelming amount of India's total subsidy payments are received by the non-poor. More than half of subsidy payments are directed to households that represent the richest 40 percent of the income ladder, and 87 percent go to households living above the poverty line. One reason for the skewed distribution is that the poorest households have relatively low electricity access rates, which prevent them from taking advantage of the tariff subsidies. However, the study confirms that a more important reason is the way in which the states' residential tariff structures and schedules are designed for BPL and APL consumers.

Notes

1. Cross-subsidies are accounted for by calculating each household's net subsidy (that is, total subsidy receipts minus total cross-subsidy expenditures), summing all net subsidies within each quintile, and dividing each quintile's total net subsidy figure by the total positive subsidy payments received by all households across all income quintiles.

2. The electricity access rate among BPL households can be further disaggregated into whether a household (i) has an available electricity connection and (ii) has chosen to connect to the grid. Because the data set in the National Sample Survey does not allow for that disaggregation, we assume that all households with available electricity connections are connected.

3. The consumption ratio is largely determined by income factors, but the state can also influence it through tariffs; for example, decreasing BPL tariffs and/or increasing APL tariffs would likely induce an increase in BPL consumption relative to APL consumption.

4. If India were to provide electricity to all BPL households and provide no new connections to APL households, it is possible that the access ratio could exceed 1.00. But that scenario is unlikely, particularly given the country's near-term goal of universal electricity access. Even if it were to pursue that strategy, the access ratio would not be significantly greater than 1.00, given the current APL access rate.

Elite Capture • http://dx.doi.org/10.1596/978-1-4648-0412-0

CHAPTER 6

Cost of Residential Subsidies

Residential electricity subsidies in India exist within the larger context of electricity-sector subsidies and cross-subsidies. Subsidized tariffs are not limited to residential consumers, but are also granted to agricultural, and in some states, commercial consumers. Generally, the distribution utilities fund some of the residential subsidies by charging cross-subsidies to industrial and, in many states, commercial consumers. To fund the remaining subsidies, the utilities receive sizeable subsidy payments from their state governments. This chapter estimates the total and state-level cost of residential electricity subsidies and the implications of reducing residential subsidies for state budgets and fiscal deficits, as well as broader, power-sector expenditures.

Cost Summary

In 2010, the gross cost of residential electricity subsidies for all states was estimated at Rs. 220,119 million, equivalent to 0.4 percent of gross domestic product (GDP) (figure 6.1). Subtracting revenue from household cross-subsidies only minimally reduces the gross cost to a net burden of Rs. 200,521 million.[1] Notably, more than two-thirds of the cross-subsidy revenue is derived from only three states: Maharashtra, Punjab, and Uttar Pradesh. Twenty states receive less than Rs. 10 million in revenue from cross-subsidies, while two (for instance, Mizoram) receive no revenue from them.

State and Power-Sector Expenditures

Reducing residential electricity subsidies has a significant potential to decrease state governments' fiscal outlays to the power sector and increase outlays for other social programs. In 2010, residential subsidies accounted for an estimated 65 percent of the Rs. 340,001 million in total state-government subsidy payments received by the distribution utilities (figure 6.1).[2] In 2012, central- and state-level public expenditures on health totaled just 1 percent of GDP, while expenditures on education represented 4 percent of GDP. Reallocating the 0.4 of

Figure 6.1 Cost of Average Electricity Subsidy and Total Distribution Subsidies, 2010

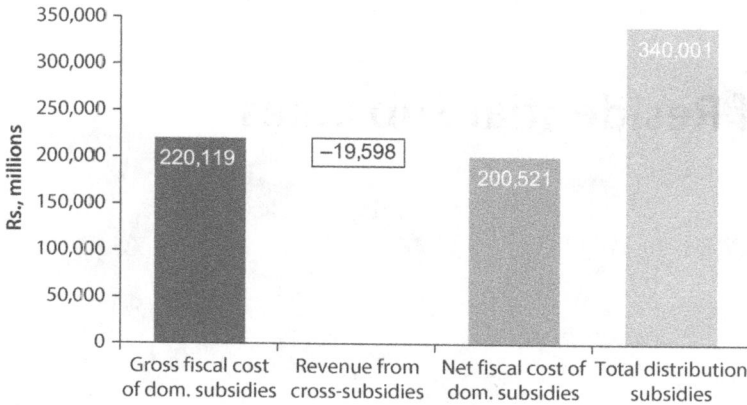

Sources: Residential subsidies and cross-subsidies (National Sample Survey 2010, PFC 2011, SERCs 2010, Planning Commission); total distribution subsidies (PFC 2011).

GDP spent on residential subsidies to health, education, or other social programs would significantly increase the size of those budgets.

Reducing residential subsidies could also decrease the electricity sector's financial losses. In 2010, residential subsidies accounted for 18 percent of the value of the electricity sector's total accumulated losses of Rs. 1,191,944 million. A portion of the utilities' subsidy requests are not fully met by state governments, which directly impacts the utilities' finances. Reducing residential subsidies would make the sector more commercially viable, which could have significant follow-on benefits (for example, enabling infrastructure investments, which would avoid such events as the 2012 blackout, and improving the quality of electricity supply).

BPL Tariff Eligibility

Estimating the cost of residential subsidies is highly sensitive to accurately identifying households as eligible for receiving below the poverty line (BPL) tariffs. As previously discussed, this study's calculations assume that all BPL and above the poverty line (APL) households are perfectly identified; however, as the literature suggests, many APL households may be inaccurately identified as BPL and vice versa (box 5.1). Figure 6.2 shows that BPL misidentification would significantly increase the fiscal burden. The per-unit subsidy would increase for some APL households and decrease for some BPL households. Because APL households consume more electricity than BPL households, the total cost of residential subsidies would increase significantly.

State-Level Cost Variations

Subsidy cost varies considerably by state (figure 6.3). In 2010, Tamil Nadu was the largest subsidizer in absolute terms; together with Andhra Pradesh it accounted for more than one-third of the net cost of subsidies. Rajasthan, Uttar Pradesh,

Figure 6.2 Cost of Average Electricity Subsidy under BPL Misidentification, 2010

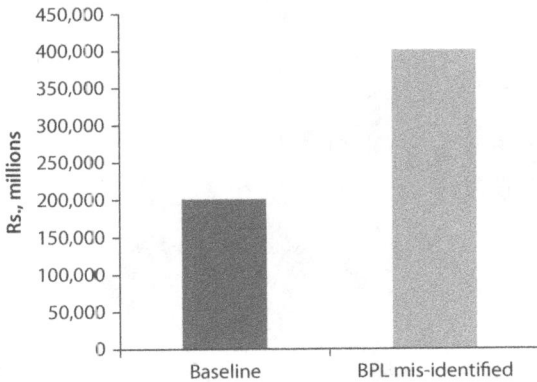

Source: World Bank.
Note: BPL = below poverty line.

Figure 6.3 Net Cost of Average Subsidy, by State, 2010

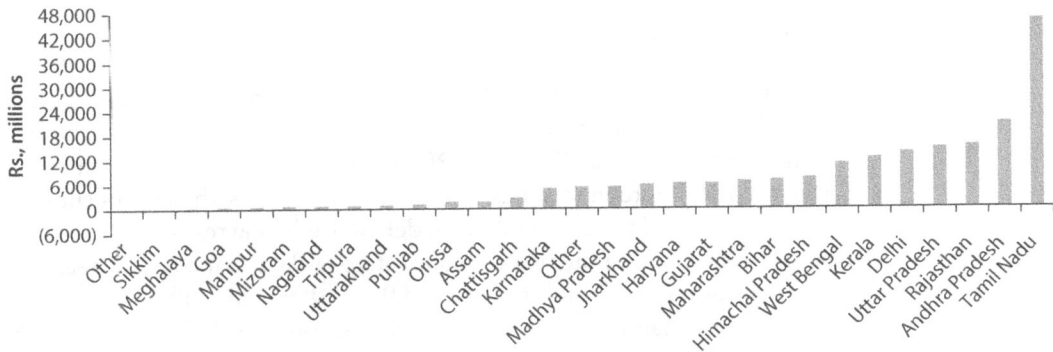

Source: World Bank.

Delhi, Kerala, and West Bengal all had more than Rs. 10 billion in net costs. At the low end of spectrum, two states including Sikkim spent the least in 2010. Sikkim spent slightly less on subsidies than on cross-subsidies, at about Rs. 15 million each, also achieving positive net revenue. Appendix G presents the gross and net cost of subsidies in absolute terms and relative to GDP for all states.

For some states, the cost of the average subsidy is significant relative to their overall fiscal deficit (figure 6.4). In Tamil Nadu and Mizoram, for example, the cost of subsidies in 2010 was equivalent to more than one-third of their respective fiscal state deficits, at 2 percent and 4 percent of GDP. In Himachal Pradesh, which has the sixth largest fiscal deficit relative to GDP, at 5.93 percent, the cost of subsidies in 2010 was equivalent to slightly more than one-quarter of that fiscal deficit. In another 10 states, the total cost of the average residential subsidy was equivalent to 10–20 percent of the fiscal deficit. For these states,

Figure 6.4 Net Cost of Average Subsidy and Fiscal Deficit as a Percentage of GDP, 2010

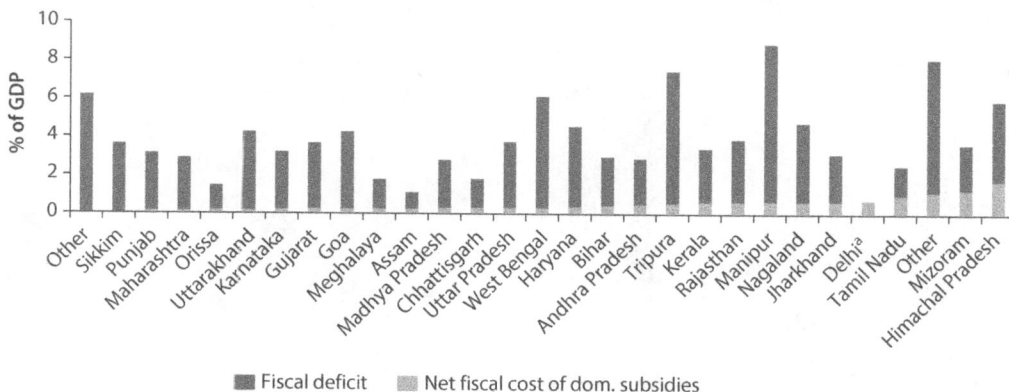

Fiscal deficit   Net fiscal cost of dom. subsidies

Sources: National Sample Survey 2010; PFC 2011; SERCs 2010; Planning Commission; RBI 2012.
a. Data on Delhi's fiscal deficit was not available.

reducing residential electricity subsidies could meaningfully reduce the fiscal deficit.

Concluding Remarks

This analysis shows that aggregate residential electricity subsidies are fairly large relative to the total subsidies that go to the power sector and power-sector losses. The misidentification of BPL and APL households plays a significant role in increasing the fiscal burden to states. For a number of states, the cost of subsidies is significant compared to the overall fiscal deficit. Reducing residential electricity subsidies has a significant potential to reduce state outlays that could be reallocated to other social programs and increase the financial viability of the distribution utilities. The next chapter considers the various options available for improving subsidy targeting and reducing costs.

Notes

1. The gross subsidy burden is estimated as the total subsidy received by the average household with electricity in each quintile in each state multiplied by the number of households with electricity in that quintile and state; this calculation applies the household electricity access rate used in this study to each state's 2010 population, assuming an average household size of 4.7 people. The net subsidy burden is calculated by using the net subsidy received by the average household in place of the total subsidy.

2. For this purpose, utilities that bundle distribution services with other electricity services are also considered distribution utilities.

CHAPTER 7

Toward Better Subsidy Performance

The Government of India has made substantial efforts to ensure that the poor have access to affordable electricity through charging tariffs below cost recovery. Yet only a small share of residential electricity subsidies are reaching below the poverty line (BPL) households, and the cost of subsidies is substantial in some states. At the same time, Indian states have a variety of available options for improving their subsidy performance. This chapter begins by summarizing subsidy performance across the country, highlighting good state practices that others can consider adopting. It then describes four model tariff structures that meet the twin medium-term policy goals of high subsidy targeting and low cost, along with the challenges most states would face in attempting to fully implement them. Finally, incremental steps are suggested for helping states to move toward achieving well-targeted, low-cost solutions.

Good Practices in India

Although all states have areas in which to improve their subsidy performance, certain states exhibit stronger performance and model good practices that other states can consider adopting. This section describes the strengths of four states, along with areas in which each can improve on performance.

High Subsidy Targeting and Low Cost

Punjab is a promising example of, achieving a relatively low cost by counterbalancing much of its subsidies with cross-subsidies; however it has ample room to improve in terms of targeting BPL consumers. Even so, it performs significantly better than other states. Assessed against the single criteria of subsidy cost, Sikkim stands out as one of the best-performing state; yet only a small portion of subsidies reaches BPL households. This approach to tariff design ensures that more revenue is taken from cross-subsidies than is paid out in subsidies and that 100 percent of subsidies target BPL households (figure 7.1).

Figure 7.1 Subsidy Targeting Rate versus Average Subsidy Cost, as a Percentage of GDP, 2010

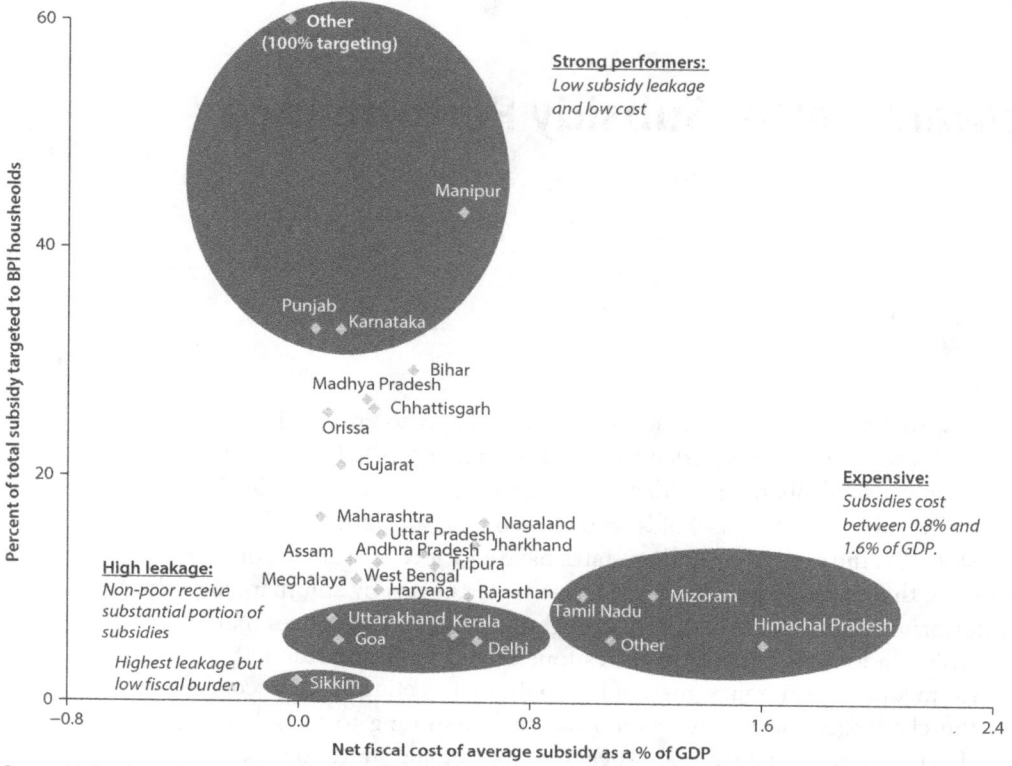

Sources: National Sample Survey 2010; PFC 2011; SERCs 2010.
Note: BPL = below poverty line.

BPL Tariff Schedule and Cross-Subsidies

Punjab achieves its strong performance by having a BPL tariff schedule—it grants free consumption of up to 200 kilowatt-hour to BPL households—and charging cross-subsidies on higher-consumption units, which offset much of the subsidy cost. At the same time, Punjab has significant room to improve on targeting. Currently, its APL schedule grants a subsidy on the first 100 units of consumption. It could consider removing that subsidy, particularly for higher-consuming households.

Sikkim achieves its low cost by limiting subsidies to households' first 50 kilowatt-hour per month and charging a cross-subsidy on all other consumption units. Because it applies the same tariff schedule to all households, every household, regardless of poverty status or total monthly consumption, receives a subsidy on its initial 50 units. This means that much of its subsidy payments are reaching APL, instead of BPL, households. It could improve its performance by creating a subsidized BPL tariff schedule and removing subsidies from the main schedule (see table 7.1).

Volume-Differentiated Tariff

Chhattisgarh follows a volume-differentiated tariff (VDT) structure, a model that all states could consider emulating. Under the VDT schedule, the state charges a

Table 7.1 Tariff Schedules in States Exhibiting Good Practices

State	Consumer group	Cost of electricity (Rs.)	Minimum bill (Rs.)	Tariff per unit of consumption (Rs./kWh) (units of consumption to which tariff applies)				
Andhra Pradesh	Single-phase, APL	2.99	28	3.45 all consumption				
	BPL		28	2.3 all consumption				
Punjab	APL and BPL with > 1 kW	3.44	35/kW	2.82	4.28	4.52		
				0–100	101–300	301+		
	BPL		0	free	4.28	4.52		
				0–200	201–300	301+		
Sikkim	All households	1.33	20 or 170 if > 5 kW	0.5	1.75	3.15	3.75	4.00
				0–50	51–100	101–200	201–400	400+
Chhattisgarh	APL	2.46	0	1.6	1.9	2.45	3.00	
				0–100	0–500	0–700	0–701+	
	BPL using < 30 kWh		0	1.5				
				0–30				

Source: World Bank.

Note: APL = above poverty line; BPL = below poverty line; kW = kilowatt.

single rate to each household, depending on its total electricity consumption. As a result, higher-consuming, often wealthier households pay the same high rate on all of their consumption. The VDT schedule allows states to grant subsidies only to lower-consuming, typically poorer households. Though targeting could be better achieved by first identifying BPL households instead of granting subsidies to low-consuming households, some of which may not be BPL, a VDT can work well when BPL households can be easily identified. At present, Chhattisgarh still has significant subsidy leakage and high cost because it grants subsidies to households consuming up to 700 kilowatt-hour per month (that is, nearly all households). By increasing tariffs on its high-consuming customers above cost, it would see notable reductions in both (table 7.1).

Meeting Medium-Term Policy Goals: Model Tariff Structures

Four model tariff structures meet the twin policy goals of high subsidy targeting and low cost: (i) creating BPL tariff schedules and eliminating subsidies from other schedules, (ii) delivering subsidies through cash transfers instead of tariffs, (iii) creating a VDT, and (iv) creating a lifeline tariff and removing subsidies from other tariffs. Deciding on which intervention is most effective depends on the strength of a state's BPL identification and cash-transfer delivery system. For states that can accurately identify BPL households, the best choices are either a subsidized BPL schedule paired with an unsubsidized APL schedule (that is, no tariffs on the APL schedule are below cost) or a cash transfer with completely unsubsidized tariff schedules (figure 7.2). States can further reduce their subsidy burden through cross-subsidies. With perfectly accurate BPL identification, either choice would have perfect targeting, and would significantly lower the cost (for example, by 4–16 percent for some BPL tariff models and by 14 percent for some cash-transfer models).

India's 2006 National Electricity Tariff Policy specifically promotes cash transfers over tariff-based subsidies; it notes:

> A direct subsidy is a better way to support the poorer categories of consumers than the mechanism of cross-subsidizing the tariff across the board…. As a substitute of cross-subsidies, the state government has the option of raising resources through [a] mechanism of electricity duty and giving direct subsidies to only needy consumers. This is a better way of targeting subsidies effectively.

Box 7.1 describes cash transfers in detail, noting the implementation issues to consider and how India's new unique identification program could be leveraged to distribute them. However, as discussed in chapter 5 (box 5.1), BPL identification is a challenge in India. Eligibility to receive BPL benefits, such as special tariff schedules, is often contingent on whether a household is a BPL cardholder. As previously discussed, studies have found that up to two-fifths of BPL cardholders are non-poor, while more than half of poor households do not have BPL cards. In this situation, the performance of both BPL tariffs and cash transfers would be compromised. The BPL tariff modeled here would direct just 19 percent of

Figure 7.2 Subsidy Targeting and Cost under Model Tariff Structures, 2010

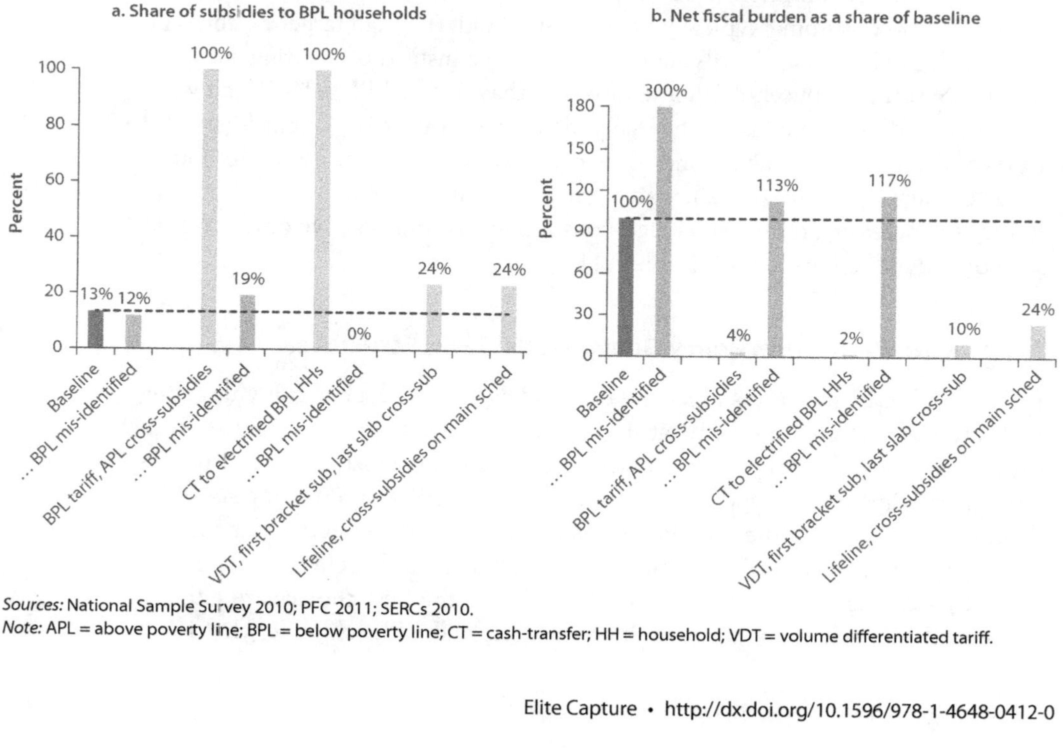

Sources: National Sample Survey 2010; PFC 2011; SERCs 2010.
Note: APL = above poverty line; BPL = below poverty line; CT = cash-transfer; HH = household; VDT = volume differentiated tariff.

subsidies to BPL households, and the cash transfer only 39 percent; both would lower cost by only half.

Until BPL households are accurately identified, states can better target poor households by delivering subsidies to households with low levels of electricity consumption, who tend to be poor, rather than BPL cardholders. States can target subsidies to low-consuming households using either a VDT, where only the lowest-consumption group receives a subsidy, or create a separate lifeline tariff for consumers under a certain consumption threshold and remove subsidies from their other tariff schedules (figure 7.2). These structures would target 24 percent of subsidies to BPL households and would reduce the cost of subsidies by 10–24 percent of the current cost or by 3–8 percent if BPL households are misidentified.

Box 7.1 Cash Transfers and India's Universal Identification System

Among all policy options for subsidy delivery, cash transfers achieve the strongest improvements in both targeting and cost reductions—comparable only to simultaneously creating a BPL tariff and removing APL subsidies. Cash transfers have been widely used in the health and education sectors to provide social protection. In some cases, they have been used to provide fuel subsidies (for example, in the Dominican Republic). But examples of using cash transfers to deliver electricity subsidies are few (for example, the Islamic Republic of Iran). In practice, it means removing subsidies from tariff schedules and delivering them instead through a cash transfer.

Cash transfers offer many potential benefits as a subsidy delivery mechanism. The government selects households to receive a transfer according to a set of criteria. This controls spending because the government chooses the size of the transfer and its recipients. Also, the government can target the recipients, allowing for a more equitable distribution of benefits than is possible through tariff subsidies. In addition, transitioning to cash transfers removes the market distortions caused by subsidies, and may help reduce energy consumption through stronger price signals.

But effective implementation of cash transfers requires careful design and strong capacity. In the Islamic Republic of Iran, for example, implementation issues may have negated many of the expected benefits for subsidy delivery (Salehi-Isfahani, Stucki, and Deutschmann 2012). Key questions include the transfer value (that is, it must be sufficiently large to make electricity affordable, yet not so large that it distorts labor markets), the unit to target (for example, individual, family, household, or electricity meter), and who in the unit should receive the transfer (for example, to manage for potential gender-differentiated impacts). In the health and education sectors, cash transfers are often conditional on specific behaviors (for example, school attendance). Because the power sector lacks such obvious conditions, cash transfers for electricity might be less feasible.

India's recently developed unique identification (UID) system offers an opportunity to overcome some of these challenges. In the past, much of India's population lacked the proper

box continues next page

Box 7.1 Cash Transfers and India's Universal Identification System *(continued)*

identification and bank accounts needed to receive cash transfers, but that is now changing. The Unique Identification Authority of India (UIDAI), a new government-sponsored program, aims to give every resident a unique national identity, which is stored electronically along with other data and is portable anywhere in India (UIDAI 2012). This program has several key advantages for identifying and targeting electricity subsidy recipients. First, it requires no physical documents for beneficiary authentication. Second, it prevents the use of duplicate or fake identities, and can transfer across states. Third, it attempts to minimize errors of exclusion by allowing UID users, at the time of enrollment, to introduce other residents who lack documentation. To pair UIDs with financial access, the UIDAI has partnered with banks to open bank accounts for UID users, which enables effective subsidy delivery. If states choose to use cash transfers rather than tariff subsidies, they could leverage the UID system, as the government is planning for some of its existing subsidy programs, potentially including fuel subsidies, scholarships, and pension benefits (Mathew and Agarwal 2012).

However, the UID system is not without its drawbacks. The full rollout of the system has met with delays, and initial attempts to deliver other cash transfers through the UID system have faced challenges. It is not yet clear whether states can effectively identify households' poverty status, which could cause continued errors of exclusion and inclusion. Similarly, it is unclear whether the system has a reliable method for tracking changes in poverty status and other demographics over time. Despite the UIDAI's financial-inclusion initiatives, the lack of financial access may persist for some time.

Source: World Bank.

Near-Term Policy Actions

Although the model tariff structures discussed above perform best, their full and immediate implementation may be a challenge for most states, particularly since they would require charging cost-recovery or higher prices to a large share of the population that currently benefits from electricity subsidies. States can instead choose to implement these models incrementally; that is, making smaller changes that tend toward improving the overall situation. There are several options for near-term policy actions. Figure 7.3 shows the impact of these changes on subsidy targeting and cost. The subsections below describe these options in detail.

Toward a BPL Tariff or Cash Transfer

The possible incremental changes in moving toward a BPL tariff or cash transfer are as follows:

1. Create a BPL tariff and leave the APL schedule unchanged;
2. Gradually reduce APL subsidies (a 50 percent reduction is modeled here);
3. Remove subsidies (that is, charge cost-recovery tariffs) from the APL schedule;
4. Add a cross-subsidy to the highest bracket of the APL schedule; and

5. Remove subsidies from tariffs entirely and give electrified BPL households a fixed cash transfer for electricity consumption (modeled here as the average subsidy currently received by a BPL household with electricity).

Creating a BPL tariff and leaving the APL schedule unchanged would improve targeting only slightly. Existing APL subsidies would continue to strongly outweigh the new BPL subsidies, given that BPL households consume significantly smaller amounts of electricity. In addition, many states already have a BPL tariff, and some already grant large residential subsidies to all electricity consumers. Thus, the impact of creating a BPL tariff would be larger in states that do not yet have one. Creating a BPL tariff without changing APL tariffs would increase the cost by introducing new subsidies, while existing ones would remain. With the reduction in APL subsidies and the addition of cross-subsidies, subsidy targeting would continue to increase, and the cost would fall. Since nearly all of India's states have large APL subsidies, the impact would be large (figure 7.3).

Figure 7.3 Subsidy Targeting and Cost under Various Incremental Tariff Structure Changes, 2010

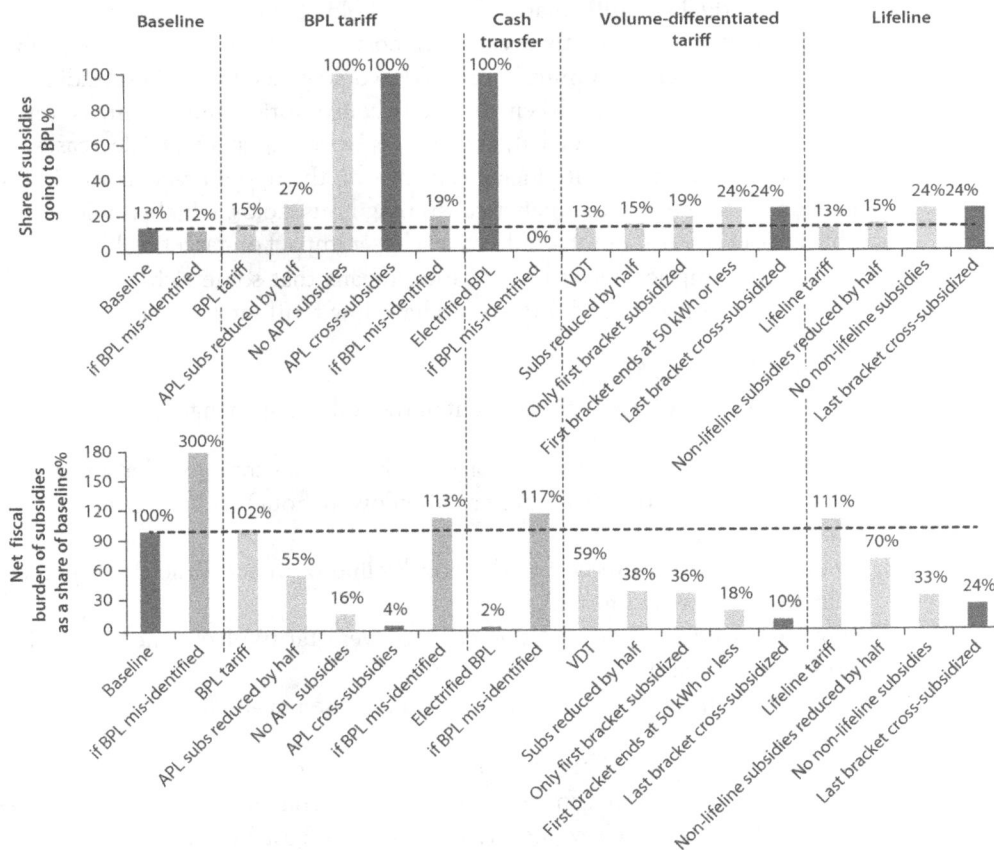

Sources: National Sample Survey 2010; PFC 2011; SERCs 2010.
Note: Darker colors represent the baseline and four model tariff structures; lighter colors are used to indicate the three sensitivity conditions. APL = above poverty line; BPL = below poverty line; kWh = kilowatt-hour; VDT = volume differentiated tariff.

Toward a VDT

Moving toward a VDT could include the following incremental steps:

1. Convert existing increasing block tariff (IBT) tariff schedules to VDT schedules, maintaining the same bracket cutoffs and tariff levels;
2. Gradually reduce subsidies for all brackets but the first (a 50 percent reduction is modeled here);
3. Remove subsidies (that is, charge cost-recovery tariffs) from all brackets but the first;
4. Lower the cutoff for the first bracket to a low level corresponding to the state's electricity-consumption patterns (modeled here as 50 kilowatt-hour); and
5. Add a cross-subsidy to the highest bracket.

Converting existing IBT tariffs into VDT tariffs would automatically exclude high-consuming households from low tariffs on initial consumption blocks. Each household would be charged the tariff that applied to the highest IBT bracket they reached.[1] Poorer households, who tend to consume less electricity, would tend to retain more of the low tariffs than richer households. Figure 7.3 shows that targeting would improve only slightly because (i) most brackets in most states are subsidized and thus higher-consuming households would generally retain subsidies and (ii) the strong correlation between electricity consumption and income is imperfect. The cost decreases somewhat, however, as switching to a VDT decreases the average subsidy magnitude. Reducing subsidies on the upper brackets would further reduce subsidies for the higher-consuming households, which would have a notable impact on cost. But it would have a lesser impact on targeting because the imperfect consumption-income correlation means that some richer households consume little electricity and thus would have low tariff rates.

Toward a Lifeline Tariff

Moving toward a lifeline tariff could entail the following changes:

1. Create a lifeline tariff schedule for households consuming under a specified level of electricity (modeled here as 50 kilowatt-hour) and leave the existing schedule unchanged;
2. Gradually reduce subsidies on the non-lifeline tariff schedule (a 50 percent reduction is modeled here);
3. Remove subsidies (that is, charge cost-recovery tariffs) from the non-lifeline tariff schedule; and
4. Add a cross-subsidy to the highest bracket of the non-lifeline tariff schedule.

Creating a lifeline tariff alone improves targeting only slightly because of the imperfect correlation between electricity consumption and income and because larger subsidies remain elsewhere. It increases the cost because new subsidies are added, while existing ones remain. By reducing subsidies for the non-lifeline brackets, targeting improves somewhat because richer households generally are not lifeline consumers. Also, the cost is lowered because subsidies are reduced. Ultimately, the cost falls quite substantially as subsidies are eventually directed only to the lowest-consuming households. But targeting is not perfect owing to the imperfect consumption-income correlation.

Shortcomings of IBT Adjustments

Gradually moving away from the current IBT structure through the steps described above—either switching to a VDT tariff structure or gradually removing all subsidies from the main IBT schedule except those for BPL or lifeline consumers—improves subsidy targeting only minimally. To illustrate how these incremental changes fall short, we consider making the following adjustments (figure 7.4):

1. Remove subsidies (that is, charge cost-recovery tariffs) from all brackets but the first;
2. Reduce the cutoff for the first bracket to 50 kilo-watt hour;
3. Charge a cross-subsidy on the last bracket;
4. Remove fixed and minimum charges (as they disproportionately increase tariffs for low-consuming households);
5. Increase tariffs by 20 percent; and
6. Achieve a 10 percent cost reduction (for example, through efficiency improvements).

Figure 7.4 Impact on Subsidy Targeting and Cost from IBT Adjustments, 2010

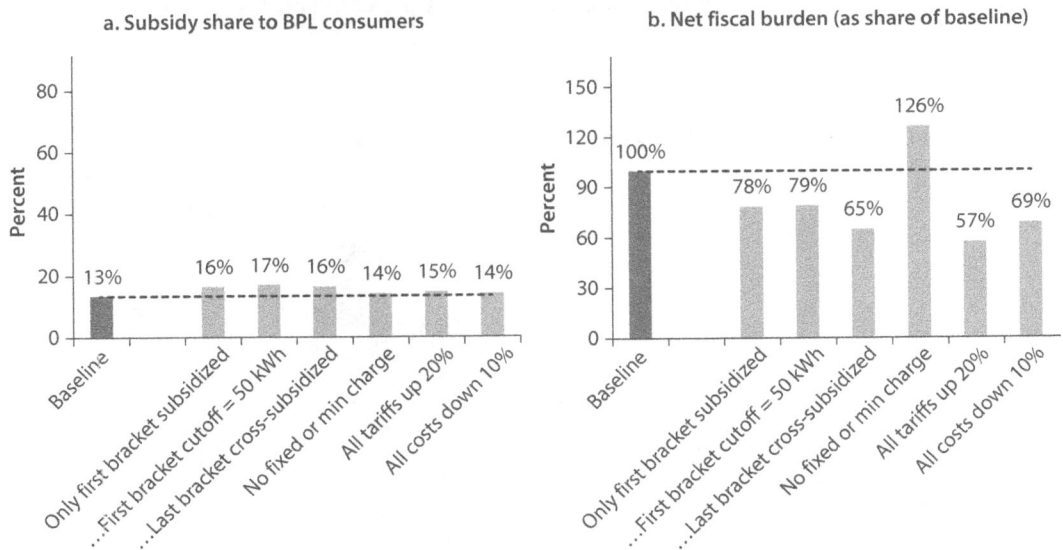

Sources: National Sample Survey 2010; PFC 2011; SERCs 2010.

None of the incremental IBT changes illustrated above significantly improve subsidy targeting. Many options are available to reduce subsidy cost, but their effect falls far short of the impact from implementing the design changes considered earlier in this chapter. IBT structural adjustments fail to significantly improve targeting because, as discussed previously, an IBT is regressive by definition. All households on a given IBT schedule are eligible for the low initial rates of consumption, meaning that households that consume more electricity, who are generally wealthier, are always eligible for more subsidies. If states choose to maintain an IBT structure, the only way to significantly improve targeting is to make one of the larger changes previously discussed (for example, adding a BPL schedule or cross-subsidies).

Increasing electricity access rates improves subsidy performance somewhat by increasing subsidy targeting. The cost of subsidies is higher, but more BPL households are enabled to receive subsidies. Figure 7.5 shows that, in the baseline scenario, 48 percent of BPL households do not receive a subsidy. The high exclusion rate is due almost entirely to the lack of electricity access among BPL households (as opposed to BPL households having access but not receiving a subsidy). As access expands, more BPL households become eligible for electricity-tariff-delivered subsidies. This expands the share of total subsidies delivered to BPL households and increases the share of BPL households that benefit from the subsidy.

Without parallel changes in tariff design, however, expansion in electricity access does little to improve subsidy targeting. Moreover, it increases the cost since subsidy recipients are added without a commensurate decrease in subsidies to currently connected households. However, if access expansion is accompanied by improvements in tariff design, subsidy targeting improves. The share of BPL households benefiting from subsidies can increase and the cost of subsidies can remain below the current cost.

Figure 7.5 Impact of Increased Electricity Access on Subsidy Performance, 2010

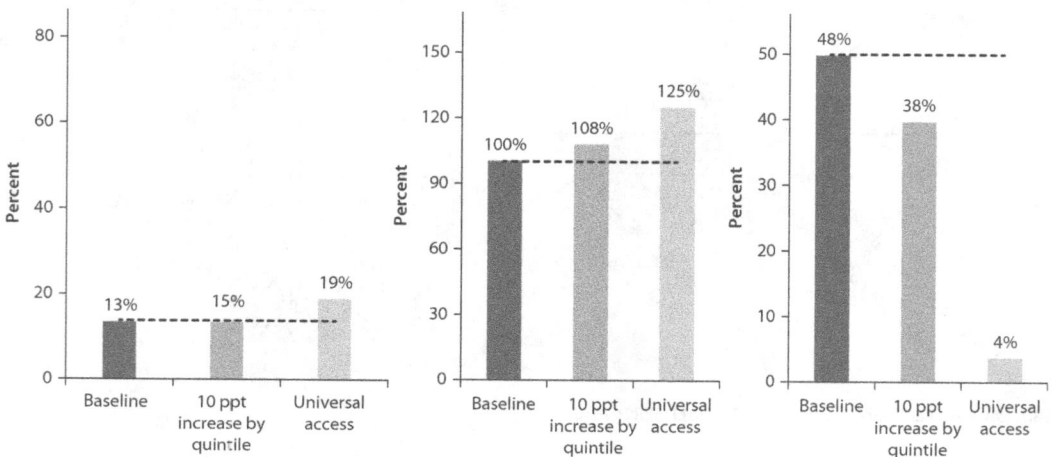

Sources: National Sample Survey 2010; PFC 2011; SERCs 2010.

Additional Considerations

Subsidy targeting and cost are regulators' two main concerns in setting tariffs. Another, perhaps equally important factor that they must consider is whether tariffs are set to promote the efficient use of electricity. Higher tariffs promote less electricity usage—an urgent need in India, given its significant supply shortage. Such additional considerations may make certain model tariff structures more attractive than others. For example, a VDT gives households a strong incentive to reduce electricity usage to avoid being pushed into a higher consumption bracket, which increases the tariff a household pays on its total consumption, not just the amount consumed in the higher bracket. Sending appropriate price signals is also an argument for using cash transfers instead of tariff-based subsidies, as recommended in India's 2006 National Tariff Policy. With a cash-transfer system, tariffs can be set only with an eye toward the efficient allocation of consumption.

Looking Ahead

Though eliminating electricity subsidies has several clear advantages, it still poses a political challenge. This study has identified the changes that India's states can make toward achieving well-targeted subsidies and transitioning to a cash-transfer system. Proceeding by incremental steps can help to make the subsidy removal feasible. Success also depends on pairing these steps with a strong communications strategy—selling the benefits of subsidy removal and alternative uses for significant fiscal savings—and a commitment to consumers that the utilities and state governments are reducing inflated electricity costs, eliminating avoidable inefficiencies, and ultimately improving electricity reliability and quality. In the current environment of frequent and prolonged power cuts and transmission and distribution losses, the utilities need to develop a creditable roadmap and begin taking steps along the path to improved electricity supply before regulators significantly increase tariffs. These actions will have the dual impact of increasing consumers' willingness to accept tariff increases and decreasing the cost that tariffs must cover.

Note

1. For example, in a state with an IBT that charges Rs. 1 for the first 100 units of consumption and Rs. 2 for the next 100 units of consumption, a household consuming 150 units would pay Rs. 1 for the first 100 and Rs. 2 for the next 50. If the IBT were converted into a VDT, that same household would pay Rs. 2 for all 150 units.

APPENDIX A

Household Electricity Consumption

State	Average monthly electricity consumption (kWh)							
				Income quintile				
	All	Urban	Rural	1st	2nd	3rd	4th	5th
Andhra Pradesh	69	101	56	43	57	65	72	106
Assam	51	63	47	27	36	43	54	65
Bihar	45	61	38	32	46	36	44	53
Chhattisgarh	64	114	52	35	37	50	69	116
Delhi	182	189	87	105	126	110	209	356
Goa	151	202	128	82	136	147	197	207
Gujarat	82	111	61	42	58	72	96	135
Haryana	91	130	72	48	65	75	86	177
Himachal Pradesh	118	159	114	96	109	113	133	140
Jharkhand	58	91	39	36	39	45	46	92
Karnataka	56	86	37	29	35	45	68	103
Kerala	77	109	66	50	60	69	87	119
Madhya Pradesh	56	95	39	31	40	48	57	93
Maharashtra	83	121	50	44	51	63	87	160
Manipur	64	64	64	63	67	65	61	62
Meghalaya	70	95	64	55	63	58	77	94
Mizoram	64	78	49	39	49	56	76	89
Nagaland	48	49	48	41	42	45	58	57
Orissa	81	105	74	48	62	71	83	101
Punjab	126	167	101	64	85	111	141	224
Rajasthan	73	108	56	51	53	56	77	113
Sikkim	43	65	39	25	43	41	52	52
Tamil Nadu	87	118	60	49	61	72	98	151

continues next page

(continued)

| | Average monthly electricity consumption (kWh) | | | | | | | |
| | | | | Income quintile | | | | |
State	All	Urban	Rural	1st	2nd	3rd	4th	5th
Tripura	46	67	40	32	33	40	45	72
Uttar Pradesh	69	102	49	44	52	51	58	103
Uttarakhand	66	98	57	55	65	71	91	48
West Bengal	59	82	44	36	40	43	54	92
Other	30	32	29	22	24	26	32	42
Other	89	124	76	72	78	83	81	127
All India	**76**	**111**	**55**	**45**	**55**	**62**	**79**	**121**

Source: World Bank.
Note: All figures are for 2010. kWh = kilowatt-hour.

Subsidy Incidence and Cost

	Percent of total subsidy payment received					Gross fiscal cost of average subsidy (Rs.)	Net fiscal cost of average subsidy (Rs.)
	Income quintile						
State	1st	2nd	3rd	4th	5th		
Andhra Pradesh	15	19	19	21	26	511,200,000	316,900,000
Assam	5	9	13	22	51	423,900,000	423,900,000
Bihar	3	7	7	26	56	275,600,000	273,254,471
Chhattisgarh	12	10	17	20	42	1,714,000,000	1,713,875,676
Delhi	8	16	22	22	32	80,285,714	26,719,716
Gujarat	0	0	0	0	0	–	(275,900,000)
Haryana	0	0	0	0	0	–	(157,900,000)
Himachal Pradesh	15	16	22	23	24	130,200,000	129,893,434
Jharkhand	3	6	10	11	71	166,100,000	164,956,687
Karnataka	9	14	16	22	38	73,962,712	(102,437,288)
Madhya Pradesh	12	8	59	8	12	10,406,236	(1,000,593,764)
Maharashtra	0	0	0	0	0	–	(2,538,000,000)
Orissa	6	13	16	25	39	112,100,000	68,850,607
Punjab	17	19	19	19	25	276,900,000	174,100,000
Rajasthan	0	0	11	10	79	1,206,398	(614,993,602)
Tamil Nadu	10	14	18	24	34	1,173,000,000	1,166,858,639
Uttar Pradesh	7	11	15	30	37	510,400,000	230,400,000
Uttarakhand	5	15	49	3	27	2,506,418	(41,545,551)
West Bengal	5	10	14	27	43	149,300,000	144,989,621
Other	14	20	19	25	21	197,500,000	197,498,246
All India[a]	**10**	**13**	**17**	**22**	**37**	**5,808,567,478**	**300,826,892**

Source: World Bank.
Note: All figures are for 2005.
a. Includes only the 20 states shown.

Average Cost of Electricity Supply and Average Effective Tariffs

State	Average supply cost (Rs./kWh)	Average effective tariff (Rs./kWh)	Gap between supply cost and tariff (Rs./kWh)
Andhra Pradesh	3.53	2.08	1.45
Assam	4.27	3.46	0.81
Bihar	4.62	2.35	2.27
Chhattisgarh	2.46	1.71	0.75
Delhi	4.97	3.23	1.74
Goa	2.86	2.16	0.70
Gujarat	3.36	2.85	0.51
Haryana	4.37	3.23	1.14
Himachal Pradesh	4.70	1.07	3.63
Jharkhand	3.80	1.60	2.20
Karnataka	3.36	2.80	0.56
Kerala	3.83	1.93	1.90
Madhya Pradesh	3.91	3.28	0.63
Maharashtra	3.68	3.38	0.30
Manipur	4.54	3.37	1.17
Meghalaya	3.26	2.66	0.60
Mizoram	6.19	2.03	4.16
Nagaland	5.25	2.68	2.57
Orissa	2.07	1.75	0.32
Punjab	3.44	3.32	0.12
Rajasthan	5.26	3.73	1.53
Sikkim	1.33	1.33	0.00
Tamil Nadu	4.26	1.35	2.91
Tripura	4.69	2.55	2.14
Uttar Pradesh	3.60	2.73	0.87

continues next page

(continued)

State	Average supply cost (Rs./kWh)	Average effective tariff (Rs./kWh)	Gap between supply cost and tariff (Rs./kWh)
Uttarakhand	3.16	2.69	0.47
West Bengal	3.55	2.26	1.29
Other	2.99	3.35	−0.36
Other	3.09	1.19	1.90
All India	**3.77**	**2.58**	**1.19**

Source: World Bank.
Note: All figures are for 2010. kWh = kilowatt-hour.

Average Subsidies and Cross-Subsidies

State	Subsidized consumption (%)	Average subsidy on subsidized electricity (Rs./kWh)	Unsubsidized consumption (%)	Average cross-subsidy on unsubsidized electricity (Rs./kWh)
Andhra Pradesh	96	1.59	4	1.59
Assam	100	0.81	0	0.06
Bihar	98	2.33	2	1.00
Chhattisgarh	97	0.78	3	0.59
Delhi	100	1.75	0	0.48
Goa	84	0.86	16	0.19
Gujarat	81	0.77	19	0.56
Haryana	99	1.07	1	2.05
Himachal Pradesh	100	3.63	0	0.17
Jharkhand	98	2.28	2	0.76
Karnataka	82	0.86	18	0.74
Kerala	94	2.08	6	0.87
Madhya Pradesh	78	0.97	22	0.58
Maharashtra	70	0.97	30	1.25
Manipur	92	1.42	8	1.84
Meghalaya	96	0.64	4	0.45
Mizoram	100	4.16	0	n.a.
Nagaland	100	2.59	0	0.57
Orissa	83	0.49	17	0.50
Punjab	59	0.83	41	0.90
Rajasthan	98	1.57	2	0.99
Sikkim	67	0.34	33	0.69
Tamil Nadu	100	2.91	0	0.74

continues next page

(continued)

State	Subsidized consumption (%)	Average subsidy on subsidized electricity (Rs./kWh)	Unsubsidized consumption (%)	Average cross-subsidy on unsubsidized electricity (Rs./kWh)
Tripura	100	2.14	0	0.12
Uttar Pradesh	73	1.34	27	0.42
Uttarakhand	89	0.75	11	1.76
West Bengal	98	1.32	2	0.28
Other	11	0.67	89	0.49
Other	100	1.90	0	n.a.
All India	**87**	**1.46**	**13**	**0.62**

Source: World Bank.
Note: All figures are for 2010. n.a. = not applicable.

Household Distribution, by Subsidy Status and Average Subsidy and Cross-Subsidy

State	Household group (%)				Average household subsidy (Rs./month)[a]	Average household cross-subsidy (Rs./month)[b]
	Full subsidy (1)	Net subsidy (2)	Net cross-subsidy (3)	No subsidy (4)		
Andhra Pradesh	97	1	1	1	104	5
Assam	99	1	0	0	41	0
Bihar	95	0	0	5	104	1
Chhattisgarh	94	0	0	6	49	1
Delhi	100	0	0	0	318	0
Goa	74	25	1	0	110	4
Gujarat	81	16	3	0	51	9
Haryana	95	0	0	5	97	1
Himachal Pradesh	100	0	0	0	429	0
Jharkhand	93	0	0	7	130	1
Karnataka	67	26	2	5	39	8
Kerala	96	3	0	1	151	1
Madhya Pradesh	88	8	4	0	43	7
Maharashtra	70	19	3	8	56	31
Manipur	85	0	0	15	84	9
Meghalaya	95	2	0	3	43	1
Mizoram	100	0	0	0	266	0
Nagaland	98	0	0	2	125	0
Orissa	63	25	2	10	33	7

continues next page

(continued)

State	Household group (%)				Average household subsidy (Rs./month)[a]	Average household cross-subsidy (Rs./month)[b]
	Full subsidy (1)	Net subsidy (2)	Net cross-subsidy (3)	No subsidy (4)		
Punjab	59	19	21	1	62	47
Rajasthan	92	1	0	7	113	1
Sikkim	34	26	6	34	9	10
Tamil Nadu	100	0	0	0	253	0
Tripura	100	0	0	0	99	0
Uttar Pradesh	81	0	0	19	68	8
Uttarakhand	80	0	0	20	44	13
West Bengal	96	3	0	1	77	0
Other	11	0	0	89	2	13
Other	100	0	0	0	169	0
All India	**86**	**7**	**2**	**5**	**101**	**8**

Source: World Bank.
Note: All figures are for 2010.
a. Households receive subsidies on at least one unit of electricity.
b. Households pay cross-subsidies on at least one unit of electricity.

Subsidy Incidence and Targeting

This annex gives state-level data on the distribution of subsidy payments by income quintile and subsidy targeting. Table F.1 provides the state-level percentages of total subsidy payments that go to each quintile. Table F.2 disaggregates the BPL targeting rate into its components (tariff design score, access score, and poverty rate). Similarly, Table F.3 disaggregates the tariff design score into its components (tariff design score, subsidy ratio, and consumption ratio).

Table F.1 State-Level Subsidy Distribution, by Income Quintile, 2010

	Total subsidy payments targeted (%)				
	Income quintile				
State	1st	2nd	3rd	4th	5th
Andhra Pradesh	15	19	22	22	23
Assam	6	9	14	26	46
Bihar	7	16	15	21	41
Chhattisgarh	10	12	16	23	38
Delhi	14	17	14	24	31
Goa	20	14	18	24	23
Gujarat	19	20	21	21	19
Haryana	12	17	19	20	31
Himachal Pradesh	17	19	19	23	22
Jharkhand	7	8	16	19	50
Karnataka	28	15	14	19	24
Kerala	15	18	19	23	26
Madhya Pradesh	13	21	22	23	21
Maharashtra	15	13	17	24	32
Manipur	16	22	20	21	21

table continues next page

Table F.1 State-Level Subsidy Distribution, by Income Quintile, 2010 *(continued)*

| | Total subsidy payments targeted (%) | | | | |
| | Income quintile | | | | |
State	1st	2nd	3rd	4th	5th
Meghalaya	14	18	16	22	30
Mizoram	9	15	18	27	31
Nagaland	17	17	19	24	23
Orissa	9	18	17	23	33
Punjab	36	14	15	16	18
Rajasthan	10	13	15	23	39
Sikkim	4	16	22	32	26
Tamil Nadu	13	15	18	23	31
Tripura	15	15	17	20	33
Uttar Pradesh	7	12	19	26	35
Uttarakhand	13	18	21	36	14
West Bengal	10	12	15	23	40
Other	82	18	0	0	0
Other	15	18	19	19	28
All India	**14**	**16**	**18**	**22**	**30**

Source: World Bank.

Table F.2 BPL Targeting Rate and Disaggregated Components, 2010

State	BPL targeting rate	Tariff design score	Access score	Poverty rate
Andhra Pradesh	0.13	0.77	0.96	0.18
Assam	0.13	0.63	0.57	0.35
Bihar	0.29	1.08	0.57	0.48
Chhattisgarh	0.26	0.64	0.91	0.45
Delhi	0.06	0.66	0.92	0.09
Goa	0.06	0.69	1.01	0.08
Gujarat	0.21	1.18	0.91	0.19
Haryana	0.10	0.65	0.91	0.17
Himachal Pradesh	0.05	0.82	1.00	0.07
Jharkhand	0.14	0.63	0.66	0.33
Karnataka	0.33	1.82	0.98	0.18
Kerala	0.06	0.76	0.94	0.09
Madhya Pradesh	0.27	0.91	0.91	0.32
Maharashtra	0.16	0.93	0.89	0.20
Manipur	0.43	1.03	0.95	0.44
Meghalaya	0.11	1.01	0.82	0.13
Mizoram	0.10	0.63	0.75	0.21
Nagaland	0.16	0.82	1.01	0.19
Orissa	0.25	1.53	0.50	0.33
Punjab	0.33	2.53	0.95	0.14
Rajasthan	0.10	0.62	0.77	0.20
Sikkim	0.02	0.25	0.73	0.09
Tamil Nadu	0.10	0.70	0.93	0.15
Tripura	0.12	1.13	0.71	0.15
Uttar Pradesh	0.15	0.82	0.58	0.31
Uttarakhand	0.07	0.73	0.91	0.11
West Bengal	0.12	0.76	0.72	0.23
Other	1.00	5.89	0.82	0.21
Other	0.06	0.80	1.00	0.07
All India	**0.13**	**0.75**	**0.72**	**0.24**

Source: World Bank.

Table F.3 Tariff Design Score and Disaggregated Components

State	Tariff design score	Beneficiary ratio	Subsidy ratio	Consumption ratio
Andhra Pradesh	0.77	0.99	1.09	0.63
Assam	0.63	1.00	1.06	0.62
Bihar	1.08	1.06	1.25	0.84
Chhattisgarh	0.64	1.00	1.05	0.57
Delhi	0.66	1.00	1.11	0.51
Goa	0.69	1.00	1.30	0.49
Gujarat	1.18	1.00	1.78	0.57
Haryana	0.65	0.99	1.07	0.52
Himachal Pradesh	0.82	1.00	1.09	0.75
Jharkhand	0.63	0.99	0.94	0.68
Karnataka	1.82	1.05	2.72	0.57
Kerala	0.76	1.01	1.17	0.61
Madhya Pradesh	0.91	1.00	1.17	0.63
Maharashtra	0.93	1.09	1.91	0.52
Manipur	1.03	1.02	1.02	0.99
Meghalaya	1.01	1.03	1.76	0.76
Mizoram	0.63	1.00	0.97	0.64
Nagaland	0.82	0.96	0.99	0.85
Orissa	1.53	1.08	2.09	0.70
Punjab	2.53	0.99	4.09	0.49
Rajasthan	0.62	0.94	0.90	0.72
Sikkim	0.25	0.41	0.97	0.76
Tamil Nadu	0.70	1.00	1.16	0.56
Tripura	1.13	1.00	1.43	0.68
Uttar Pradesh	0.82	0.99	0.92	0.89
Uttarakhand	0.73	0.84	1.30	0.86
West Bengal	0.76	1.00	1.11	0.63
Other	5.89	5.89	1.00	1.00
Other	0.80	1.00	1.02	0.80
All India	**0.75**	**1.01**	**1.25**	**0.59**

Source: World Bank.

Gross and Net Fiscal Cost of Average Subsidy

State	Gross fiscal cost of average subsidy		Net fiscal cost of average subsidy	
	(Rs.)	%	(Rs.)	%
Andhra Pradesh	22,080,000,000	0.45	21,045,600,000	0.43
Assam	1,656,000,000	0.18	1,655,802,893	0.18
Bihar	7,032,000,000	0.40	6,980,943,456	0.39
Chhattisgarh	2,604,000,000	0.26	2,553,112,368	0.26
Delhi	13,800,000,000	0.62	13,799,957,291	0.62
Goa	427,200,000	0.14	409,536,276	0.14
Gujarat	7,464,000,000	0.17	6,156,000,000	0.14
Haryana	6,216,000,000	0.28	6,134,310,072	0.28
Himachal Pradesh	7,536,000,000	1.60	7,535,989,899	1.60
Jharkhand	5,880,000,000	0.61	5,846,688,276	0.61
Karnataka	6,144,000,000	0.18	4,908,000,000	0.14
Kerala	12,480,000,000	0.54	12,414,513,576	0.53
Madhya Pradesh	6,360,000,000	0.28	5,298,000,000	0.23
Maharashtra	15,000,000,000	0.17	6,672,000,000	0.07
Manipur	525,600,000	0.63	469,577,772	0.56
Meghalaya	270,000,000	0.20	262,275,752	0.20
Mizoram	648,000,000	1.23	648,000,000	1.23
Nagaland	658,800,000	0.64	658,101,518	0.64
Orissa	2,040,000,000	0.12	1,603,200,000	0.10
Punjab	4,380,000,000	0.22	1,080,000,000	0.05
Rajasthan	15,600,000,000	0.59	15,433,200,000	0.59
Sikkim	14,554,056	0.03	(387,588)	0.00
Tamil Nadu	46,440,000,000	0.98	46,439,986,841	0.98
Tripura	720,000,000	0.47	719,837,023	0.47
Uttar Pradesh	16,800,000,000	0.32	14,856,000,000	0.28

continues next page

(continued)

State	Gross fiscal cost of average subsidy		Net fiscal cost of average subsidy	
	(Rs.)	%	(Rs.)	%
Uttarakhand	1,089,600,000	0.16	765,600,000	0.12
West Bengal	11,052,000,000	0.27	11,006,196,852	0.27
Other	5,108,202	0.01	(26,962,554)	−0.04
Other	5,196,000,000	1.08	5,196,000,000	1.08
All India	**220,118,862,258**	**0.36**	**200,521,079,724**	**0.33**

Source: World Bank.
Note: All figures are for 2010.

Bibliography

Ahmed, F., C. Trimble, and N. Yoshida. 2012. "The Transition from Under-Pricing Electricity in Bangladesh: Fiscal and Distributional Impacts." World Bank, Washington, DC (mimeo).

Banerjee, S., V. Foster, and Q. Wodon. 2010. "Dealing with Poverty and Inequality." In *Africa's Infrastructure: A Time for Transformation*, edited by V. Foster and C. Briceno-Garmendia. Washington, DC: Africa Development Forum, Agence Française de Développement, and World Bank.

Foster, V., S. Pattanayak, and L. S. Prokopy. 2003. *Do Current Water Subsidies Reach the Poor?* Washington, DC: World Bank.

Fukumi, Atsushi. 2012. "Political Economy of Government Expenditures: A Case of Power Subsidy in India." *The BRICs as Regional Economic Powers in the Global Economy*. Sapporo, Japan: Slavic Research Center.

Guillaume, D., R. Zytek, and M. R. Farzin. 2011. "Iran—The Chronicles of the Subsidy Reform." IMF Working Paper, International Monetary Fund, Washington, DC.

Komives, K., V. Foster, J. Halpern, and Q. Wodon. 2005. *Water, Electricity, and the Poor: Who Benefits from Utility Subsidies?* Directions in Development. Washington, DC: World Bank. http://siteresources.worldbank.org/INTWSS/Resources/Subsidybook.pdf

Krishnaswamy, S. 2010. "Shifting of Goalposts—Rural Electrification in India: A Progress Report." Vasudha Foundation, Bangalore, India.

Mahamallik, M., and G. B. Sahu. 2011. "Identification of the Poor: Errors of Exclusion and Inclusion." *Economic and Political Weekly* XLVI (9)(February 26).

Mathew, Liz, and Surabhi Agarwal. 2012. "UPA's Cash Transfer Scheme to Boost UID." Live Mint (and the *Wall Street Journal*), November 30. http://www.livemint.com/Politics/XU18B3c4xV314yifhElbGM/ UPAs-cash-transfer-scheme-to-boost-UID.html.

National Sample Survey. 2010. http://mospi.nic.in/Mospi_New/site/inner.aspx?status=3&menu_id=54.

Pargal, Sheoli, and Sudeshna Ghosh Banerjee. 2014. *Delivery of Reliable Power in India: The Challenge of Distribution*. Washington, DC: World Bank.

PFC (Power Finance Corporation Ltd.). 2011. *The Performance of State Power Utilities for the Years 2007–08 to 2009–10*. New Delhi: Power Finance Corporation Ltd.

Planning Commission. 2007. *Poverty Estimates for 2004–05*. New Delhi: Government of India, Planning Commission, March.

———. 2012. *Press Note on Poverty Estimates, 2009–10*. New Delhi: Government of India, Planning Commission, March.

Prayas Energy Group. 2011. "Rajiv Gandhi Rural Electrification Program: Urgent Need for Mid-Course Correction." Discussion Paper, July.

Ram, F., S. K. Mohanty, and U. Ram. 2009. "Understanding the Distribution of BPL Cards: All-India and Selected States." *Economic and Political Weekly* XLIV (7) (February 14).

Rao, N. D. 2012. "Kerosene Subsidies in India: When Energy Policy Fails as Social Policy." *Energy for Sustainable Development* 15: 35–43.

RBI (Reserve Bank of India). 2012. "Handbook of Statistics on the Indian Economy." March 12.

Salehi-Isfahani, D., B. W. Stucki, and J. Deutschmann. 2012. "The Impact of Iran's Subsidy Reform on Households: Evidence from Survey Data" (mimeo).

Saxena Committee Report. 2009. "Identification of BPL Households in Rural India." Report of the Expert Group to advise the Ministry of Rural Development on methodology for conducting the Below Poverty Line (BPL) Census for 11th Five Year Plan. http://www.scribd.com/doc/ 19960255/Saxena-Committee-Report-on-Poverty-Estimates-in-India- (last accessed January 14, 2012).

Trimble, C., and S. Redaelli. 2012. "An Analysis of the Distribution and Cost of Electricity Subsidies in the Maldives." World Bank, Washington, DC (mimeo).

Trimble, C., N. Yoshida, and M. Saqib. 2011. *Rethinking Electricity Tariffs and Subsidies in Pakistan"* Washington, DC: World Bank.

UIDAI (Unique Identification Authority of India). 2012. "Aadhaar-Enabled Service Delivery." Government of India, Planning Commission, Unique Identification Authority of India.

Zhang, F. 2009. *Distributional Impact Analysis of the Energy Price Reform in Turkey.* Washington, DC: World Bank.

Environmental Benefits Statement

The World Bank is committed to reducing its environmental footprint. In support of this commitment, the Publishing and Knowledge Division leverages electronic publishing options and print-on-demand technology, which is located in regional hubs worldwide. Together, these initiatives enable print runs to be lowered and shipping distances decreased, resulting in reduced paper consumption, chemical use, greenhouse gas emissions, and waste.

The Publishing and Knowledge Division follows the recommended standards for paper use set by the Green Press Initiative. Whenever possible, books are printed on 50 percent to 100 percent postconsumer recycled paper, and at least 50 percent of the fiber in our book paper is either unbleached or bleached using Totally Chlorine Free (TCF), Processed Chlorine Free (PCF), or Enhanced Elemental Chlorine Free (EECF) processes.

More information about the Bank's environmental philosophy can be found at http://crinfo.worldbank.org/wbcrinfo/node/4.

green
press
INITIATIVE